LivingOn

LivingOn

PORTRAITS OF TENNESSEE SURVIVORS AND LIBERATORS

A Project of the Tennessee Holocaust Commission
Photographs by Robert Heller

The University of Tennessee Press • Knoxville

Copyright © 2008 by The University of Tennessee Press / Knoxville.
All Rights Reserved. Printed in China.
First Edition.

This book is printed on acid-free paper.

Library of Congress Cataloging-in-Publication Data

Living on : portraits of Tennessee survivors and liberators : a project of the
Tennessee Holocaust Commission / Photographs by Robert Heller. — 1st ed.
        p. cm.
Includes bibliographical references and index.

ISBN-13: 978-1-57233-623-0 (hardcover: alk. paper)
ISBN-10: 1-57233-623-4 (alk. paper)

 1. Jews—Tennessee—Biography.
 2. Holocaust survivors—Tennessee—Biography.
 3. Soldiers—Tennessee—Biography.
 4. World War, 1939–1945—Concentration camps—Liberation—Personal narratives.
 5. Tennessee—Biography.
 I. Heller, Robert.
II. Tennessee Holocaust Commission

F445.J5L58 2008
940.53180922768—dc22
[B]   2007047105

CONTENTS

PREFACE   ix
    Gilya Gerda Schmidt

ACKNOWLEDGMENTS   xv
    Felicia Anchor and Ruth K. Tanner

INTRODUCTION   xix
    David Patterson

PHOTOGRAPHER'S NOTE   xxxix
    Robert Heller

PORTRAITS OF TENNESSEE SURVIVORS AND LIBERATORS

    Herta Adler   2

    Ethel Berger   4

    Mark Blank   6

    Clark Blatteis   8

    Olga Borochina   10

    Wallace F. Carden   12

    Leonard Chill   14

    Rachel Gliksman Chojnacki   16

    Jack Cohen   18

    Frances Cutler   20

    Henrietta Diament   22

    Ruth Diamond   24

James F. Dorris Jr. 26

Trudy Naumann Dreyer 28

Sonja Dubois 30

Robert Eisenstein 32

Joseph Exelbierd 34

Henry Fribourg 36

Jack Fried 38

James Garner 40

Jimmy Gentry 42

Zina Gontownik 44

Matilda Steinberg Goodfriend 46

Willie Hall 48

Hanna Hamburger 50

Julian Joseph Hosnedl 52

Fred Jarvis 54

Nina Katz 56

Paula Kelman 58

Ida Frank Kilstein 60

Jacob Kilstein 62

Mira Ryczke Kimmelman 64

William Klein 66

Yakov Kreymerman 68

Frida Landau 70

Elizabeth Limor 72

Menachem Limor 74

Esther Loeb 76

Herman Loewenstein 78

Hedy Lustig 80

Robert Mamlin 82

Nessy Marks 84

Rose Marton 86

George Messing 88

Helene Messing 90

Roman Mitelman 92

Olivia Newman 94

Max Notowitz 96

Reva Oks 98

Arthur Pais 100

Robert Ray Jr. 102

Eric Rosenfeld 104

Eva Rosenfeld 106

Fridericka Saharovici 108

Leonid Saharovici 110

Raymond Sandvig 112

Alexander Savranskiy 114

Gertrude Schlanger 116

Ralph Schulz 118

Jack Seidner 120

Erika Sigel 122

Ella Silber 124

Lea Slomovic Naft and Sara Slomovic Seidner 126

Harry Snodgrass 128

Paula Stein   130

Sol Stein   132

Hans Strupp   134

Raisa Terk (Kreymerman)   136

Simon Waksberg   138

Frieda Weinreich   140

Sam Weinreich   142

Fred Westfield   144

Dee Wolfe   146

Henry Wolkoff and Sally Abramczyk Wolkoff   148

INDEX   151

PREFACE

The Tennessee Holocaust Commission (THC) was called into being by Governor Lamar Alexander in 1984 to educate Tennesseans about the Holocaust. Having served on the commission for the past ten years, I can attest that we are an enterprising, if eclectic, group of individuals who are determined to get out the message. We have done so in many different ways—through organizing annual workshops for middle school and high school teachers, honoring outstanding teachers of the Holocaust with the annual Belz-Lipman Award, taking groups of teachers to the United States Holocaust Memorial Museum, and underwriting various other projects, including educational trips for teachers to the concentration camps in Europe, Holocaust conferences throughout the state, teacher resource trunks containing a variety of multimedia educational tools, and periodic traveling exhibitions. The commission's most recent such project was an exhibition focusing on Holocaust survivors and liberators who reside in Tennessee. Known as "Living On: Portraits of Tennessee Survivors and Liberators," this exhibit has been traveling to venues in the state and neighboring Kentucky since April 2005.

How does a project like this come into being? Usually, it takes the fortunate confluence of a variety of necessary factors: the idea, the resources, the expertise, and the interest of the public. We were blessed to have all of those at the right time. I don't remember exactly who had the idea of chronicling all of the still-living Tennessee survivors and liberators, but the minutes of the August 15, 2002, THC teleconference reflect a line item (number 26) for the "Survivor Photograph Project." The urgency of documenting these heroes of an event that happened more than half a century earlier was apparent to everyone on the commission, and indeed we lost identified participants even before they could be photographed and interviewed—and unfortunately are losing more continuously. But how to go about it? We were very fortunate in that respect. In 1995, when the THC underwrote the first Holocaust Conference in Knoxville, sponsored by the Fern and Manfred Steinfeld Program in Judaic Studies at the University of Tennessee,

Associate Professor Robert Heller from the UT College of Communications contacted me with the idea of exhibiting survivor photos that he had taken in Miami in the 1980s. We took him up on the idea, and many of the viewers of the exhibition commented on the creativity of the project—their stories were inscribed on the panels around their portraits—and on the powerful expressions on their faces. The Jewish community in Knoxville invited Rob to display the portraits for our Yom HaShoah commemoration one year, and in 2001, when we organized a second Holocaust Conference, I again asked Rob to contribute his Miami survivor portraits. This time he hung them in midair, at eye level, on the first floor of Hodges Library on the UT campus. The exhibition created a stir. We kept a guest book that we later presented to Rob, and he was touched by the many moving comments from viewers. So, when the project of the Tennessee survivors and liberators was first discussed at the Tennessee Holocaust Commission, the question of who would do it, usually a big one, was clear to those of us on the commission who had seen Rob's Miami survivor portraits. And we suggested during that August 15, 2002, meeting that the exhibition, once completed, might also be turned into a book.

We agreed that first things had to come first. The commission invited Professor Heller to submit a proposal for this photographic project, and we budgeted twenty thousand dollars for the undertaking. The objective was "to create a traveling exhibit for the state of Tennessee that can be accommodated in communities of different sizes." We expressed the hope "to personalize the project with stories of Tennesseans and help individuals learn about the Holocaust through these personal accounts and the face to face meeting of survivors through their photos." One interesting aside is that we did not yet have any conception of the project's scope. When Felicia Anchor, our commission chair, explained that this project was still in the planning stages, she was not exaggerating. The minutes of the October 2002 meeting reflect that the commission expected the exhibition to be "smaller than the Luboml exhibit," a photographic portrait of a prewar Jewish community in Poland, which we had contracted for and which had traveled around the state in 2001. How wrong we were! While the Luboml project had given us invaluable experience in putting an exhibit on tour, we had not actually developed the art and other materials for that exhibition ourselves, and as we would see, the number of images ultimately produced for "Living On" would prove to be significantly larger than the number involved in the earlier exhibit. We were clearly moving into new territory.

When I speak of the commission as enterprising, much of the credit has to go to Felicia and to Ruth Tanner, our executive director, as well as to Stacey Knight, our administrative assistant, who manages much of our day-to-day business. In December 2002 they sprang into action, writing and submitting a grant proposal for "the survivor portrait project" to the Conference on Jewish Material Claims Against Germany, Inc., in New York for 50 percent of the anticipated cost. In addition to contracting with Rob Heller for the photographic aspect of the project, the commission also asked Dawn Weiss Smith, a contributing writer to the *Jewish Observer* in Nashville, to conduct interviews with the survivors. A December 23 memorandum from Ruth to the board of directors asserted confidently, "We expect to begin no later than March 2003."

And so it was. In 2003, the annual State Observance of Yom HaShoah at the State Capitol occurred on April 29. The spring commission meeting was timed to coincide with that date. Rob Heller and Dawn Smith were invited to make a presentation to the commission concerning the project. During final pre-project discussions with Felicia and Ruth, a schedule was mapped out for the interviews and photography, which would happen in two large waves that same year—in East Tennessee in April and May and in Middle and West Tennessee from June through August. Again, the bold conclusion in the minutes stated, "Our goal is to showcase the exhibit for Yom HaShoah 2004."

But where to find the appropriate individuals? Ruth contacted all Jewish federations and Jewish community center directors as well as all Tennessee rabbis to request their support and assistance. In the Spring/Summer 2003 edition of *The Flame,* the THC's newsletter, a column on page 5 announced, "THC Seeks All Tennessee Survivors and Liberators," explaining that the "THC is soliciting assistance in locating every Holocaust survivor and concentration camp liberator who lives in Tennessee to take part in a photography/biography portrait project." In addition, the Tennessee Press Association arranged for Ruth Tanner to write a brief article to disseminate to their member newspapers. The Veteran's Oral History Project, an undertaking of the U.S. Archives, through regional interviewing sites such as the Nashville Room of the Nashville Public Library and the Gore Center at Middle Tennessee State University, yielded further names of liberators to contact. How to determine who is a survivor and who a liberator? The commission came up with this definition: "THC considers survivors to be anyone living in Europe after *Kristallnacht* (November 1938). Liberators are those who fought to liberate a concentration camp or who visited a death or concentration camp within 30 days of its liberation." Later, the liberator definition was expanded to include U.S. Army witnesses, particularly those present at the Nuremberg Trials. And so the work began.

On July 17, 2003, the directors and commissioners received an ecstatic email from Ruth: "We had some very good news today! I placed a call to the Claims Conference and was informed that we have been awarded a grant for 'Living On: Portraits of Tennessee Survivors and Liberators' in the amount of $16,000!" Mazel tov! As of that date, fifty-eight people had been signed up to be photographed and interviewed in Bristol, Knoxville, Chattanooga, Nashville, and Memphis. By the time of the October 2003 THC meeting, forty-four interviews had been done across the state. The expected final number of participants was estimated to be sixty-five. We still did not yet have any real sense of the exact nature of the exhibition, causing one commissioner to inquire what the project would look like.

It was at this time that we learned of Will Pedigo's participation in the project. Will is an associate producer for WNPT, the public television station in Nashville. He was a former student of Rob's at UT. Will, Ruth told us casually, "has been taping the process of the interviews." This was an understatement, as would only become apparent in 2005 when Will edited down his fifty-five hours of tape into a one-hour program, which was creatively interspersed with music he composed, as well as with music by the Klezmer band "Tennessee Schmaltz," with whom Rob plays. On April 18, 2005, Nashville Public Television premiered the documentary, "Living On: Tennesseans Remembering the Holocaust," which subsequently received a regional Emmy for best documentary.

In December 2003, the commission's e-newsletter informed everyone that "in mid-November, Rob and Dawn completed the remaining interviews in Nashville and Memphis that were not documented this summer. The turnout was extraordinary. In three intense days they met with twenty-one people, some of whom were unknown to us before the project received widespread coverage in area newspapers this summer." The final tally was seventy-four.

And for the first time, we got a sense of what the project would look like. Ruth reported, "Rob produced two prototype photographs as a preview. The images are magnificent." It could not have been said better. At this time, also, the name of Susan Knowles, a Nashville-based professional museum curator, was first mentioned. The commission made plans to preview the "Living On" exhibition at the 2004 State Observance of Yom HaShoah on April 20. As our January 2004 e-newsletter announced, "We are arranging for a select group of images and their accompanying biographies, representing all the regions of the state, to be on display in the Capitol as well as a special guest speaker to acknowledge the project's launch."

After the state observance and before the spring meeting in Memphis on May 17, the Frist Center for the Visual Arts in Nashville was first mentioned as a possible venue for the exhibition in spring 2005. The impact of this possibility could be seen in the agenda for the May 17 meeting, when the language of the "Living On" agenda item spoke of "an exhibit for museums," in addition to other public spaces and school classrooms. The notion of a "museum quality exhibition" was again stressed in the meeting minutes, which reported that "99% of the photographs and interviews have been completed within the past twelve months." The challenge then became one of getting "our project out to the state of Tennessee." It was the fortunate collaboration between the commission's curator, Susan Knowles, and the experts at the Frist in Nashville, led by curator Mark Scala, which brought the project to a final form that proved immensely effective and compelling in presenting the stories of Tennessee survivors and liberators to all Tennesseans. The text panels that accompanied each portrait, as well as the introductory panel and map panels, which were created by an independent graphic artist, Amy Donaldson, were of superb quality, greatly enhancing the powerful photographic images.

In explaining the impact of a strong portrait, Rob Heller has noted, "It is sometimes said that if you look into someone's eyes long enough, you can see into that person's soul." Tennesseans in Nashville, Memphis, Chattanooga, Clarksville, Knoxville, Dickson, Johnson City, and Jackson, as well as residents of western Kentucky, have had a chance for a personal encounter with the souls of those who experienced the Holocaust firsthand, either as victims or as American soldiers.

The idea of creating a book of the photographs was there from the beginning, but one has to set priorities. Having the individuals photographed and interviewed while there was still time was the top priority, and getting the images out to the public was the next. Now that many Tennesseans have seen the power of the spirit in these individuals, it is time to preserve them for posterity, for our children, grandchildren, and great grandchildren, so that they, too, will never forget. We hope that they remember not only the inhumanity of groups driven by an irrational hatred for others but also the determination of the persecuted to live, the resiliency of the human soul, and the compassion of the Allied soldiers who seemed godlike to the victims at the same time that these liberators experienced unspeakable torment from their encounters. All of this and more can be learned from the photographs and stories in this volume.

GILYA GERDA SCHMIDT
Professor and Head,
Department of Religious Studies
Chair, Fern and Manfred Steinfeld
Program in Judaic Studies
University of Tennessee

ACKNOWLEDGMENTS

For twenty-five years, the Tennessee Holocaust Commission has sought numerous and different approaches, through public programs and teacher seminars, to add meaning to the events of the Holocaust that helps personalize this history. In its efforts to encourage further remembrance and education, creating tangible personal connections remains a haunting challenge.

While our goal always has been to transmit the history of the Holocaust in this way, a comprehensive means to achieve this goal did not become a plan of action until early 2003. In that fertile spring, the idea for *Living On: Portraits of Tennessee Survivors and Liberators* was born.

Because the Tennessee population of survivors and liberators and other U.S. Army veterans who witnessed the horrors of Nazi genocide firsthand is relatively small—a number we felt we could embrace—creating a photography-biography project seemed feasible. What we did not know at first, but recognize now with reverence, is the breadth and variety of experiences the interview project would reveal. In fact, our microcosm turned into a macrocosm that not only reflected diverse refugee and survivor accounts but also distinct liberator, U.S. Army witness, and political prisoner histories.

Every location within the state to which the exhibition traveled in the first two years brought requests for additional interviews from individuals who either did not know about the project or who, after seeing the beauty and power of the exhibition, wanted their stories included. These additions added to the richness of the whole.

This success gave us the freedom to consider yet another format to showcase this unique Tennessee story: a book that would hold within its covers the *Living On* images and histories.

Why is a book about *Living On* important to the Tennessee Holocaust Commission? Unfortunately, there will be a day when no firsthand witnesses will be able to recount their experiences. Like the exhibition, a book stops time and permits those interviewed to give their testimony. Like the exhibition, a book allows Tennesseans to meet their neighbors in ways that are otherwise unknown and unanticipated.

A book would have its own personality and significance, creating a permanent tactile connection between the reader, the images, and their companion stories. The reader would recognize the value of holding this history, quite literally, in one's own hands. There is something extraordinary in this relationship between book and reader, a relationship that exists in spite of the wonders of modern technology.

Through *Living On: Portraits of Tennessee Survivors and Liberators,* the Tennessee Holocaust Commission has been able to fulfill its mission to a degree that seemed unimaginable in its earliest years. Through *Living On,* the history of the Holocaust and the individuals who lived that history are honored, and their legacy is transmitted to new generations. These stories and faces are now yours to reflect upon and carry forward.

The Tennessee Holocaust Commission approached this project as a novice. Through our network within the state, however, we discovered a treasure trove of talent. Without the energy and assistance of these dedicated and experienced people, *Living On* as an exhibition, a documentary film, a Web site, and now a book would not have been possible. It is only because of the caring expertise of those whose names are listed below that the richness of this endeavor was realized. To them, as well as to the members of the Tennessee Holocaust Commission, we owe our most profound thanks.

FELICIA ANCHOR, COMMISSION CHAIR
RUTH K. TANNER, EXECUTIVE DIRECTOR
Tennessee Holocaust Commission

Living On Exhibition

Robert Heller, associate professor, School of Journalism and Electronic Media, the University of Tennessee; photographer

Dawn Weiss Smith, interviewer and writer

Susan W. Knowles, curator, text editor, and supplementary interviewer

Amy Donaldson, graphic designer

Will Pedigo, documentary filmmaker; associate producer, Nashville Public Television

Living On Web Site

J. Seth Johnson, assistant professor of graphic design, Middle Tennessee State University

Amy Haywood, graduate student, Middle Tennessee State University

Gwynn Thayer, archivist, Tennessee State Library and Archives, artifact captioning and content editor for video segments

Living On Teacher Seminars

Ronda Robinson, *Living On* Teacher Resource Book, text editor

Arlene Samowich, graphic designer

Andrea Steele, *Living On* Discussion Guide, writer

Paul Fleming, principal, Hume-Fogg Academic Magnet School, Metropolitan Nashville Public Schools, presenter

Sue Chaney Gilmore, Martin Luther King Magnet School, Metropolitan Nashville Public Schools, presenter

Jan Hatleberg, Meigs Magnet Middle School, Metropolitan Nashville Public Schools, presenter

Griff Watson, adjunct faculty, Tennessee State University and United States Holocaust Memorial Museum Regional Educator, presenter

SPECIAL THANKS

Mark Scala, exhibition curator, and Lauren Thompson, editor, Frist Center for the Visual Arts, Nashville, and the design and production team at the Frist whose foresight and creativity brought the original exhibition to fruition

Stacey L. Knight, administrative assistant for the Tennessee Holocaust Commission, who coordinated all aspects of the project

Anne Plummer, who proofread the manuscript

The Conference on Jewish Material Claims Against Germany for its funding support

The University of Tennessee Press

INTRODUCTION

On April 26, 1986, a cloud of radioactive material rose into the air from a chimney at a nuclear power plant in Chernobyl. Two weeks later, radiation levels in Montana were up. In fact, we can determine air pollution levels for any given year by examining a plug of snow and ice from Antarctica. Which means: an event that takes place in one part of the planet can affect the entire planet in very literal, very graphic ways.

During the Holocaust, the smoke from burning Jewish bodies billowed into the air not for one day but for a thousand days, not from one chimney but from dozens. The winds have spread the ashes of those millions of Jewish men, women, and children over the face of the earth. Which means: the remains of the murdered inhabit the soil from which we harvest our grain. They abide in the bread we put into our mouths. They become part of the very fabric of who we are, body and soul. That is why the Holocaust will not go away. It is an inescapable part of our physical and spiritual being. It haunts our conscience and our consciousness from within.

How could this reality that exceeds possibility have happened? How could the calculated extermination of the Jews of Europe have taken place in the heart of European Christendom?[1] How could it have been conceived and implemented by the preeminent heirs to the Enlightenment? When we turn to history for answers to these questions, I would argue, we collide with a devastating revelation: the Holocaust happened precisely because the Jews were trapped in the heart of European Christendom, where they fell prey to a certain strain of the thinking of those heirs of the Enlightenment.

Historical Background

The hatred for the Jewish people that paved the way to Auschwitz has its roots in the early centuries of Christianity. It is true that anti-Judaism existed prior to the advent of Christianity.

With the spread of the message of the Gospels, however, anti-Semitism took on a theological dimension. Although the Church fathers never called for the extermination of Jews, many of them did not hesitate to heap scorn on the children of Abraham. According to Saint Ambrose (ca. 340–397 C.E.), bishop of Milan, it was not a crime to burn synagogues. Saint John Chrysostom (347–407) described the Jews as enemies of God and was among the first to accuse the Jews of deicide. While Saint Augustine (354–430) recognized the Jews as witnesses to the truth of the Hebrew Scriptures, he viewed their exile as a divine punishment for rejecting Christianity.

Despite this preaching of hatred, there was no mass murder of the Jews until the launching of the First Crusade in 1096, when thousands of Jews were slaughtered in the Rhineland. The massacres in the time of the Crusades were followed by widespread slaughter of the Jews in England in 1190, in Germany in 1348–49, in Poland and the Ukraine in 1648–49, and in the 1880s and 1903–6 in Russia. During the centuries following the Crusades, new accusations were made against the Jews. The first blood libel arose in Norwich, England, in 1144, leveled by William of Norwich, who later attained the title of saint; he alleged that the Jews were responsible for the murder of a young boy and that Jews conducted this ritual murder, reminiscent of the crucifixion, under the guidance of an international Jewish conspiracy centered in Narbonne. By the late thirteenth century, the charge spread to the continent, where the blood libel was attached to the accusation that the Jews used the blood of Christian children to make their matzot for Passover and even as an aphrodisiac. Further, the Jews were said to be agents of Satan, desecrators of the Host, sorcerers, and vampires. In 1290, the Jews were expelled from England, in 1394 from France, in 1420 from Austria, in 1492 from Spain, in 1496 from Portugal, in 1512 from Provence, and in 1569 from the Papal States. Indeed, at one time or another, Jews were expelled from almost every country in Europe.

While one might suppose that the dawn of the Enlightenment in the eighteenth century would bring more tolerance toward the Jews, it was just the opposite: during the Age of Reason, the philosophical anti-Semitism of the intellectuals was added to the theological anti-semitism of the Christians. Nearly all of the great philosophers of the eighteenth and nineteenth centuries—including Voltaire, Immanuel Kant, Johann Gottlieb Fichte, G. W. F. Hegel,

Arthur Schopenhauer, and Friedrich Nietzsche—delivered diatribes against the Jews. It turns out that, in part, the Holocaust happened not because of any breaking away from the ideas of the Enlightenment, but precisely because the Nazis' chief instigators were so thoroughly versed in the German intellectual and cultural history that emerged from the Enlightenment. Because they were so familiar with the philosophical texts of the Enlightenment, they were able to exploit the anti-Semitic portions of those texts to suit their own murderous ends.

At the opening of the June 1939 meeting of the National Socialist Association of University Lecturers, Professor Walter Schultze declared, "What the great thinkers of German Idealism dreamed of . . . finally comes alive, assumes reality."[2] Emphasizing the self's autonomy, authenticity, and resolve, the German Idealism that arose in the Enlightenment and contributed to the Holocaust follows a clear line of development from certain elements of the philosophy of Kant (1724–1804) onward. Taking the Jews to be the embodiment of a "slave mentality" because they follow commandments from God, and not from their own reason, Kant declared that "the euthanasia of Judaism is the pure moral religion."[3] After Kant came Hegel (1770–1831), who developed a view of God that ultimately denies the otherness of the divinity. In the end, this would mean that the ego is divine. Thus, the thinking that situates the self at the center marginalizes both God and neighbor. In the thought of the Neo-Hegelian Ludwig Feuerbach (1804–1872), God becomes merely a projection of one's psyche.[4] By the time we get to Nietzsche (1844–1900), the God of Abraham is dead,[5] and other human beings are mere *Untermenschen*.

In Nietzsche's view, the will to power is a will to freedom, and freedom is understood as an autonomy beyond any law, resolute and decisive. In keeping with this line of thought, Martin Heidegger (1889–1976) insisted that human authenticity lies in human resolve, for resolve is the height of one's freedom and autonomy. It means that what is mine is mine not by right but by determination. It means that what is mine is mine, and what is yours is mine—which, says the Talmud, is a manifestation of evil (see *Pirke Avot* 5:10). It is, indeed, the Nazi evil. Thus, it should come as no revelation that Heidegger, perhaps the most influential philosopher of the twentieth century, was a card-carrying, unrepentant Nazi.

I would contend that a certain line of thinking that began with Kant's Idealism and culminated in Heidegger's nihilism has to seek the elimination of the Jew, since the Jew embraces the absolute authority of the Holy One, who is known only through His uncompromising commandments. The Nazis' annihilation of the Jews and Judaism was not simply a case of scapegoating or racism run amok. In keeping with a major line of philosophical development from Kant onward, the Nazis sought the destruction of the God of Abraham and everything He signifies through the destruction of God's chosen. It is perhaps startling but certainly not surprising, then, to discover that by 1940 nearly half of the philosophers of Germany were members of the Nazi Party.[6]

Without this history of the theological and philosophical animosity toward the Jews, I believe, one cannot begin to understand the history of the Holocaust.

On November 9, 1919, one year after the First World War had come to a close, the Weimar Republic was born. Disgruntled and disillusioned over Germany's loss of the Great War, many joined anti-Semitic right-wing groups such as the Thule Society. In September 1918, the German Army sent a corporal to investigate the suspicious organization. He was so taken by it that he decided to join it himself. In January 1919, the society founded the German Workers' Party. By the time they took the name National Socialist German Workers' Party on February 24, 1920, the now-discharged corporal was the party's leader. His name was Adolf Hitler.

In the parliamentary elections of 1920, the National Socialists—or Nazis—won 14 (or 3 percent) of the Reichstag's 459 seats. In November 1932, they won 196 (or 34 percent) of the Reichstag's 572 seats. On January 30, 1933, Hitler was appointed chancellor of Germany. The survivors and liberators whose names and faces appear in this powerful volume are all too familiar with the history that ensued.

By the end of March 1933, several concentration camps were in operation, including the one in Dachau where Matilda Goodfriend, Arthur Pais, and William Klein were sent. By 1939, numerous other camps had been opened, including Buchenwald (1937), where Menachem Limor was liberated by American GIs such as Harry Snodgrass, and Mauthausen (1938), where Paula Stein, Henry Wolkoff, and Sally Abramczyk Wolkoff endured the unspeakable. Even more camps would soon be added to this list, with names like Natzweiler (1940), another camp that Matilda Goodfriend endured; Theresienstadt (1941), where Frida Landau arrived after ten days of living on grass; Stutthoff (1942), where Zina Gontownik was sent; and Bergen-Belsen (1943), from which Henrietta Diament, Mira Kimmelman, and Ruth Diamond were finally rescued.

Then there were the six camps whose primary purpose was the extermination of the Jewish people and whose death factories were in operation by the spring of 1942: Chelmno, Sobibor, and Treblinka, where Menachem Limor's mother and brother were gassed and burned; Majdanek, where Henrietta Diament was separated from her husband before being sent to Auschwitz; and Belzec, the camp from which Max Notowitz escaped while being transported there. And, of course, there was the most infamous death camp of them all: Auschwitz-Birkenau, where Simon Waksberg and Mira Kimmelman arrived on transports with half of the deportees dead by the time they reached the camp—the very trains that carried Jews to the gas chambers were themselves instruments of extermination. In Auschwitz-Birkenau, Gertrude Schlanger lost her entire family, Henrietta Diament and Frances Cutler lost their mothers, Sonja Dubois lost her parents, Nina Katz lost her parents and grandfather and sister, Helen Messing lost her father, and Erika Sigel lost her mother and four brothers. It is a camp survived by Rose Marton, Frieda Weinreich, Sam Weinreich, and many others whose stories are told here.

These are not just the names of terrible places on the map of the Nazi anti-world. Their names and their unreal reality are etched into the faces that look back at us from these pages.

All of it began with the transformation of the law. Everything the Nazis did to the Jews in Nazi-occupied Europe was "legal." In Hitler's Germany, there was no concept of an unjust law, for only a concept of the human being as one whose value is derived from something sacred—and not from something contingent, such as race—can determine that a human law may not be in keeping with a higher law. Thus, on April 7, 1933, it became illegal for Jews to work for the government. As of April 21, 1933, Jews could no longer perform ritual slaughter. In September 1933, a series of laws were passed that prohibited Jews from working in art, literature, theater, and film. On October 4, 1933, Jews were banned from journalism. On September 15, 1935, the Nuremberg laws, which codified the definition of a Jew, were passed. Under those laws, anyone with one Jewish grandparent could be labeled a Jew; as for the grandparent, he or she was anyone who was a member of a synagogue. Further, under those laws,

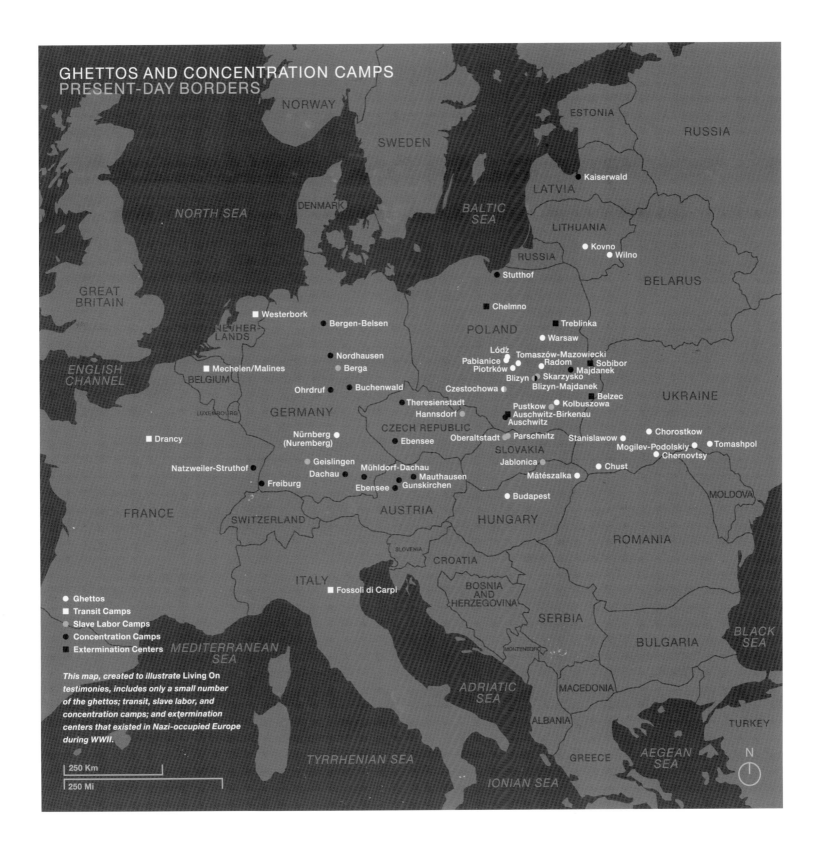

GHETTOS AND CONCENTRATION CAMPS
PRESENT-DAY BORDERS

NORWAY

NORTH SEA

SWEDEN

DENMARK

BALTIC SEA

ESTONIA

RUSSIA

LATVIA

● Kaiserwald

LITHUANIA

RUSSIA

● Kovno ● Wilno

BELARUS

GREAT BRITAIN

● Stutthof

ENGLISH CHANNEL

□ Westerbork

NETHERLANDS

● Bergen-Belsen

● Nordhausen

□ Mechelen/Malines

● Berga

BELGIUM

LUXEMBOURG

● Ohrdruf ● Buchenwald

GERMANY

■ Chelmno

POLAND

■ Treblinka

● Warsaw

Łódź ● Tomaszów-Mazowiecki
Pabianice ● Radom ● Sobibor
Piotrków ● Majdanek
Blizyn ● Skarzysko
Blizyn-Majdanek

● Czestochowa

■ Belzec

UKRAINE

● Theresienstadt
Hannsdorf

Pustkow ● Kolbuszowa
Auschwitz-Birkenau
Auschwitz

□ Drancy

Nürnberg (Nuremberg)

CZECH REPUBLIC

● Ebensee

Oberaltstadt ● Parschnitz

● Stanislawow

● Chorostkow

● Tomashpol

Mogilev-Podolskiy ● Chernovtsy

● Natzweiler-Struthof

● Geislingen

Mühldorf-Dachau

Jablonica

● Chust

● Freiburg

Dachau

Ebensee ● Gunskirchen

● Mauthausen

Mátészalka

FRANCE

SWITZERLAND

AUSTRIA

● Budapest

HUNGARY

MOLDOVA

ROMANIA

SLOVAKIA

SLOVENIA

CROATIA

ITALY

□ Fossoli di Carpi

BOSNIA AND HERZEGOVINA

SERBIA

BULGARIA

BLACK SEA

● Ghettos
■ Transit Camps
● Slave Labor Camps
● Concentration Camps
■ Extermination Centers

MEDITERRANEAN SEA

ADRIATIC SEA

MACEDONIA

MONTENEGRO

This map, created to illustrate Living On *testimonies, includes only a small number of the ghettos; transit, slave labor, and concentration camps; and extermination centers that existed in Nazi-occupied Europe during WWII.*

ALBANIA

GREECE

TURKEY

AEGEAN SEA

250 Km

250 Mi

TYRRHENIAN SEA

IONIAN SEA

N

anyone who had converted to Judaism was deemed a Jew. And so we see that with regard to the Jews, the Nazi position was not reducible to racism.

In keeping with the premise that there is no law above the word of the Führer, on February 10, 1936, the Gestapo was officially determined to be Hitler's direct instrument and allowed to operate without judicial oversight. On January 26, 1937, Jews were prohibited from working as accountants, teachers of German children, and dentists. The Aryanization of all Jewish property began in October of that year. After the Evian conference of July 5, 1938, when twenty-nine countries met and decided to do nothing about the growing Jewish refugee problem, the Nazis concluded that they had been given a green light. On October 5, 1938, they revoked the passports of all German Jews, and on October 28, they sent seventeen thousand Polish Jews back to Poland. Perhaps the most infamous instance of how the world had closed its doors on the Jews is the case of the ship *St. Louis,* whose 937 Jewish refugee passengers set sail from Hamburg on May 13, 1939, only to be turned away from Havana and Miami and then sent back to what would become Nazi Europe. Clark Blatteis was on that ship.

The first organized, massive assault on the Jews came on November 9, 1938, the notorious *Kristallnacht,* or the "Night of Broken Glass," when 30,000 Jews were arrested, 267 synagogues were burned, and 7,500 Jewish shops were looted throughout Germany. Herta Adler remembers the synagogue in flames in her little town of Diez. It was the night when six-year-old Trudy Naumann's grandmother's feet were cut by the broken glass from the shattered window just above the bed where they slept in the small Bavarian town of Unsleben.

Not long after the war began with the invasion of Poland on September 1, 1939, the first ghetto was established in Piotrków on October 28, 1939, a ghetto that Jacob Kilstein knew only too well. On April 30, 1940, the longest-standing ghetto, the Lodz Ghetto, was sealed, as was the Warsaw Ghetto on November 15 of that same year. The ghettos were not places to "live," or merely a means of isolating Jews for deportation to the extermination camps. Rather, they were also instruments of extermination, where the legal food ration was about 225 calories per day, and the occupancy level was about eight people per room. Rachel Chojnacki's story illustrates this point very well: she and her family shared a two-room apartment in the Lodz Ghetto with a dozen other people. And Leonard Chill remembers living in the Wilno

(Vilna) Ghetto with "four or five families to a room." When the Germans invaded Russia on June 22, 1941, the Final Solution was underway. On July 31, 1941, Hermann Göring ordered Reinhard Heydrich to proceed with plans to work out the logistics of exterminating the Jews of Europe. In compliance with that order, on January 20, 1942, Heydrich convened the notorious Wannsee Conference. The mass deportations from the Warsaw Ghetto to Treblinka began on July 22 of that year.

In the end, more than six million Jews, including more than a million and a half children, were forever wiped off the face of the earth.

The Essence of the Holocaust

Thus the facts. But what do they mean? "We knew who the Germans were," says Nina Katz. But who were they?

To answer this question, let us begin with the Nazi ideologue Alfred Rosenberg, who insisted that the Aryan "race has been poisoned by Judaism,"[7] and not merely by Jewish blood, for the "ism," he maintained, is *in* the blood. The Nazis targeted the Jews not because some Jews prospered during an economic depression; otherwise it would have been enough to impoverish them. Nor was it because they were an easy scapegoat for social problems; otherwise it would have been enough to rid only Germany of its Jews. It was because the Jewish presence in the world signified a testimony—a Torah—concerning the absolute sanctity of every human being. Such a teaching, so fundamental to Torah, was fundamentally at odds with Nazi thinking.

In the Nazi worldview, the Jews were not an economic or political or social problem but a cosmic, existential evil that had to be eradicated. Nazi ideology maintains that the value of the human being lies in an accident of nature: if a person happens to be born a so-called Aryan, he or she has more value than one who is not born an Aryan. Within the category of Aryan, those who have the greatest will to power have the greatest value. Such a fundamental ideological principle cannot abide in the same universe with the fundamental principles of Judaism and the Jewish view of the value of a human being. The Nazis, I contend, were not anti-Semites because they were racists; rather, they were racists because they were anti-Semites.

According to the centuries-old teaching of the Jewish people, the Holy One creates every human being in His own image and likeness. Therefore, the value of a human being lies outside of anything that can be weighed, measured, counted, or observed. The notion of holiness tells us that the value of a person is determined by nothing that is in the world, nothing that belongs to accident or circumstance. Holiness circumvents all circumstance. Further, Judaism teaches that all humanity has its origin in a single human being, in Adam, and that each of us is bound to the other both through blood and through a common tie to God. Nothing could be more threatening to Nazi ideology. And nothing could be more in keeping with *Living On,* as we begin to understand when we hear Max Notowitz declare, "I have and gain a lot of strength from Judaism. In every way it is who I am." And so we see what the Nazi anti-Semite is "anti" about.

The Nazis' calculated assault on the divine spark within the human being is part of the singularity of the Holocaust; it is a distinctive aspect of the Nazis' singular assault on Jews and Judaism. Undertaking the extermination of the Jews, the Nazis set out to destroy the very notion of something holy, of something beyond both personal will and natural accident, that abides at the core of humanity. They understood all too well that both the Source and its seekers, both God and His witnesses, had to be destroyed.

Assaulting the Holy One, the Nazis planned their actions against the Jews according to the Holy Calendar. In fact, there was a grim joke among the Jews of the Warsaw Ghetto: if we can last for twenty-one days, we can make it—the twenty-one holy days in the annual cycle. The massive deportations from the Warsaw Ghetto to Treblinka began on Tisha B'Av, the day that commemorates the destruction of the Temple, first in 586 B.C.E. by the Babylonians and later by the Romans in 70 C.E., for the Nazis understood that the burning of the body of Israel amounted to the burning of the Temple, the center of the emanation of the light unto the nations. By degrees it became illegal to observe the Sabbath, to study Torah, to pray, to put up a mezuzah, to use a ritual bath, to get married, to have children, to bury the dead, or to wear a beard, as Olga Borochina recalls. "To be caught with a pen or paper [in the ghetto]," remembers Mira Kimmelman, "would mean instant death." And, says Frieda Weinreich, "Synagogues were burned down; schools for Jewish children were destroyed."

Among the Nazis' first targets were old people and children—the two favorite disguises of the Messiah, according to Jewish tradition. The murder of the children was especially horrendous. "They would come in and murder the children for one stupid made-up reason or another," Nessy Marks remembers from her time in the Kovno Ghetto. Paula Kelman recalls, "I was twelve when my sister cut my long pigtails and applied rouge to my lips. I instantly became eighteen when the Nazis asked my age. It saved my life." Zina Gontownik remembers how the Nazis loaded Jewish children into a truck, threw them into ditches, and set them aflame. With this burning of the bodies of the little ones, it was as though creation itself had gone up in flames. For all of creation, says the Talmud, is sustained by the breath of little children (*Shabbat* 119b). It is their lips that carry our prayers to God's ear, for their lips are untainted by sin.[8] When the Nazis rendered entire areas void of children, it was as if they had rendered God deaf to the cries of the Jews. It was as if God were dead.

Because the crime of the Jew was existing in the world, the most heinous criminal was the one who brought the Jew into this world: the mother. Thus, the Nazis undertook an assault on the mothers of Israel, which was also an assault on God, for the Midrash teaches that the Torah enters this realm only through the mothers of Israel (see *Mekilta de-Rabbi Ishmael, Bachodesh* 2), and the Talmud teaches that blessing enters a home only through a woman (*Bava Metzia* 59a). Therefore, we have the image that Dachau liberator Robert Mamlin will never forget: "Half-buried women holding babies, their pitiful rags tossed aside. They thought they were going to the showers and someone would launder their clothes . . . but they were gassed. They were just mothers holding their children in the showers. They had no idea."

Another manifestation of the Nazis' assault on the image of the Holy One within the human being is their assault on the name—for the soul is made of the name. It is part of God Himself, who called the Name. The assault can be seen not only in replacing the name with a number when the Jews entered a camp, but also in placing the Jews in situations in which, if they wanted to live, they had to change their names, as happened to Leonard Chill, Frances Cutler, Sonja Dubois, and Fed Jarvis. The tearing of the name from the soul took its first concrete form in 1938, when the Nazis added the name *Israel* to every Jewish male and the name *Sarah* to every Jewish female in Germany. Collapsing the name of every Jew into the same name amounts to rendering every Jew nameless. Thus, in the former we have the obliteration of the name of a people (Israel), in the latter the obliteration of their origin (their mother Sarah). In both we have an assault not only on the Jews of Germany but also on the Name Himself. In presuming to name the Jews of Germany, the Nazis took their first step toward the usurpation of the Name, as if to say, "You think the God of Israel has named you? You are wrong: *we* have named you."

This assault on the name—on the soul and on the God who names the soul—is most fundamentally an assault on the face, which is the embodiment of the very humanity recaptured in this volume of names and faces. The great sage of the Talmud, Rabbi Akiba, maintains that the humanity and dignity of the human being are revealed in the face; in the face lies the image and likeness of the Holy One,[9] which is most fundamentally manifest in the prohibition against murder. The Nazi must obliterate the face of the Jew, for the Nazi's aim is to eliminate the absolute nature of the prohibition against murder.

The face, however, not only forbids us to kill—it commands us to open the door, offer a word of encouragement, and do any number of small, mundane things for the sake of another. And yet, like every act of kindness, the face is laden with mystery. When the Nazis assault the holy within the human, the mystery and the meaning of the face are obliterated in a twisting and torturing of the face. One means of attaining this twisting was to render the Jew *shamefaced,* both in the eyes of others and in the Jew's own eyes. So we see yet another dimension of the Nazi assault on the soul: it was not the perpetrator, not the murderer, who was ashamed but his victim. The hole these Jews burrowed into swallowed up their humanity, because what was buried in that hole which resembles a grave is the human face.

Along with shame, there was the sorrow and the terror that became not just transitory emotions but the defining features of the Jewish face. Thus it happened that Jews could be recognized not only by the insignias on their sleeves, but by the sorrow implanted on their faces, a sorrow that continues to cast its shadow over the faces of the survivors portrayed here. In the time of the Holocaust, as the assault on the faces of the Jews ran its course, their faces were gradually emptied of every expression of life that animates the face. Drained of life, Jewish faces lost their animation to a death that disfigured them before they were dead, making the Jewish face into nothing more than a breathing death mask. And so we begin to sense the depth of the miracle captured in *Living On,* in these faces that harbor not only the shadow of death but, more profoundly, an affirmation of life. Returning to life, however, had its challenges.

Difficulties Facing the Survivor

Here we come to perhaps the most difficult part of this introduction, for here we come to the issue of liberation. As of the Evian Conference, the world had turned a blind eye to the Jews. From the silence of the Vatican to the indifference of the Allies, it would remain, for the most part, blind. No one went into Europe with the cry, "Let's save the Jews!" And so, strictly speaking, the camps were not "liberated"—they were stumbled across. This fact takes nothing away from the awesome courage of the GIs who came across the camps. Indeed, for most of them— even for those who had survived the carnage of Normandy and numerous other battles—what they saw in the camps was their most traumatic experience of the war.

"Inmates everywhere," Harry Snodgrass recalls of his entry into Buchenwald. "Some dead and some alive under the dead . . . just lying there. I couldn't think. No thoughts came to my head. Only horror. I had never seen anything like this before." Veteran James Garner, speaking of what he saw as a liberator of Dachau, says, "War brings terrible things to us all, but this was different." James Dorris was also among the Americans who were first to reach Dachau: "I had never seen what despair really looked like until that day." Another GI witness who entered Dachau was Robert Eisenstein. "People were still there," he says. "They looked at us. We looked at them. Hollow." We learn that, for Robert Ray, who was among the liberators of Nordhausen, "sixty years later, he can still see their faces." Willie Hall, another soldier who liberated Nordhausen, sums it up: "I had horrible nightmares . . . nightmares for a very long time."

As horrific as the trauma was for the liberators, however, it was far more so for the survivors. All too often the difficulty facing the survivors was a matter of people being unwilling to believe or afraid to listen. They had emerged from the "concentrationary universe"[10] with a testimony and a message they could not deliver. The Nazi evil and the souls of their murdered families cried out from within them, but they could not make themselves heard. Jacob Kilstein, for example, recalls his efforts to share his tale and transmit his message. "It just tears my heart," he says, "that for many years, when we were willing to share, begging to talk, no one cared. I suppose I am glad they hear us now. But many died not having been heard. They deserved this time to speak—more than anyone else." And so we come to a startling realization: the soldiers are not the only ones faced with the task and the responsibility of liberating the Nazis' victims. We who receive their words also have a share of responsibility for their liberation. These messengers from the anti-world return to the world to transform us into messengers. "I made it my mission to tell the world," declares Nina Katz. And, says Esther Loeb, "We have a commitment and promise to fulfill." To refuse these survivors an ear is to refuse them their return to life; it is tantamount to denying the fact of the Holocaust itself.

Many of us do not want the survivors to be liberated because then we would have to listen to them. We do not want to listen to them because their testimony harbors questions that implicate us in our own responsibility, in our own humanity. The survivors speak, and from beyond their words comes the first question put to the first human being: where are you? And we do not want to hear it. Even the liberators face the problem of a liberation from their liberation of the camps. For Harry Snodgrass, "the hour at Buchenwald became six decades of nightmares." And so, just as we are summoned to listen to the survivors, so are we summoned to listen to their liberators. For both, the fear expressed in the nightmares that haunt them is a fear of the failure of liberation, the fear that once you are inside Auschwitz or Buchenwald or Mauthausen there is no getting out.

The survivors and their liberators did not merely experience the Holocaust; rather, the Holocaust "experienced" them—it became part of their essence and their experience ever after. They left the concentrationary universe, but they did not leave it behind: the prisoner, especially, was not in Auschwitz—Auschwitz was in the prisoner. "This is an indelible mark," the tattooed number on the arm declared. "You will never leave here." Through the needle, Auschwitz invaded the flesh and stained the image of the human being; through the flesh, it entered his soul and substance. Liberation from the concentrationary universe came not only with the breaking down of the prison gates but with the opening up of a path to follow. If that path had been erased, then there could be no liberation. When the gates marked *Arbeit Macht Frei* were unlocked, most of the prisoners did not move, for they had nowhere to go. That is one difference between the survivors and the liberators: the liberators at least had homes and families to return to, as difficult as it surely was.

Having lost a home to return to, the Jews were faced with a movement of return that they could not even initiate. To be liberated from the anti-world meant leaving it behind, in the past, so that the past, present, and future of life's time might be regained. But the survivor would remain contemporary with Auschwitz: it would not be left behind, and the passing of the years yielded no past. Listening to these survivors' tales, one gets the impression that something other than the survivor speaks in their memory, that in this memory lurks a voice with which the voice of memory constantly struggles. It is a possession for which there is no exorcism.

Liberation would entail a liberation from the dominating voice of the *it* of Auschwitz. With the obliteration of the name and the face, the Jew is turned over to the nondescript *it*—a pronoun without an antecedent. "No one was really free," says Jacob Kilstein. "Not when you have lost your family, your life, and all that you knew." Freedom, then, seemed all but impossible. "World news told of Jewish liberation," Ethel Berger remembers, "but freedom was bittersweet." The world news of freedom suggested an image of life diametrically opposed to the survivor's own image as one who has lived through her own death; for the survivor, time had collapsed, leaving her outside. Brave American soldiers, like Dee Wolfe, opened the gates. But they could not show the prisoners the way out. Neither they nor anyone else could offer the understanding or explanation that might place a closure on the event. Neither they nor anyone else could return the home and its sacred center to the survivors. Neither they nor anyone else could free the survivors from the death that overtook them before their lives were over. There is no getting the horror "off their chest" because it is curled up in their souls. Where indeed, then, is the liberation?

And so we find that, for the survivor, engagement with life is a departure from the camps; for us, engagement with the camps—engagement with the survivor's collection of portraits and testimonies—is a departure from life. And yet, despite everything, most survivors, like the ones portrayed here, found a place among the living. They had children, made careers, and took up residence in a world finally willing to hear what they had to say. Whereas a collection of portraits such as this one would have been inconceivable forty years ago, it comes to us now in the twilight of these remarkable lives. For good or for ill, the Holocaust has found its way into popular culture through film and television; since more of us are now willing to listen, more survivors are willing to speak. There are scholars and teachers, artists and agents, ready to write books and articles about them, teach courses on them, make movies about them, and arrange speaking engagements for them. Those who have spoken in the twilight of memory have as their contexts a Holocaust Remembrance Day and memorial museums dedicated to the message they are trying to transmit. There are workshops and conferences, professional appointments and professional organizations, devoted to Holocaust studies.

But there is also the increase in anti-Semitism and Holocaust denial throughout the world. Since more of us either ignore or deny the event, more survivors sense the urgency to speak. Perhaps most significantly, many survivors now have grown children who have asked them to tell their tale. Some survivors see their lives drawing to a close and want to speak before they die; others finally take up the struggle in the war against memory to engage yet again the Angel of Death. Once the victims of the Nazi assault on the soul, the survivors are now the victims of time and the fading of memory that comes with time. And they are faced with transmitting a fading memory. Thus Nina Katz's determination to "keep that memory alive." Whereas survivors once faced the problem of either fear or denial among those to whom they offered their memories, they now face the problem of retrieving those memories. And so they wrestle with the Angel of Forgetfulness. And, as they engage the Angel, so do we.

The Importance of This Work

We have seen the problem of liberation that confronts both the survivors and their liberators, the problem of surviving and of finding some liberation—the problem of living on. And yet the survivors of the Holocaust, as well as the liberators, miraculously lived on. That they did so is history's most penetrating testimony to the capacity of the human soul to affirm life, contrary to every reason and rationale to say no to life. And that history, that testimony that concerns all humanity, has found its way into Tennessee. The reader who picks up this book soon becomes more than just another reader, for this is not just another book. Poring over the pages of this extraordinary work is a matter of life and death. It is a matter of determining whether the survivors and liberators brought before us shall live on, whether their memories and their names shall live on. Indeed, peering into these eyes and listening to these testimonies are part of a sacred task that each of us must undertake if we are to see the post-Holocaust world live on—and if we are to live on.

In these images, in these words, of the Holocaust survivors and liberators of Tennessee, we have a microcosm of a world, or rather of two worlds: the anti-world of death and the true world of life after death. Nor is it merely about them, as if the rest of us were free from the unrest that haunts these people, these faces, since the Nazi onslaught. The Holocaust was unprecedented in its scope and singular in its implications. It cut a wound into the body of all of Israel, of all humanity, and not just those who fell prey to the catastrophe. The *Midrash Chinukh* says that if a single human life is taken, the victim's blood raises an outcry that reverberates throughout the universe.[11] What, then, must be the outcry of a sea of blood? The cry, indeed, is deafening.

Few volumes dealing with the capacity of the human being to affirm the dearness of life in the aftermath of massive death run deeper than this collection of the words and the faces of survivors and liberators who lived on after the Holocaust, for few events in human history so profoundly negated the dearness of the human being. That is why the Holocaust was so devastating both for the survivors and for their liberators: when the amazingly courageous GIs entered the remnants of the Nazi concentration camps, they came face to face with a humanity that had endured history's most devastating assault on the very meaning of humanity.

Photographer Robert Heller has done the impossible: he has seized a lifetime in an instant and a world in a face. If there have been people who shied away from the camera for fear that it would capture their soul, Heller has justified their fear. For in these portraits of Tennessee Holocaust survivors and liberators we collide with souls radically wounded in the world's most radical assault on the soul. And yet these souls live on. That too is a miracle. That too is a manifestation of the impossible conveyed in these portraits. Gazing into these eyes that gaze into us, we step before the countenance, and we are transformed into witnesses. Those eyes overflow with the humanity that the Nazis set out to erase. These portraits reveal the depth dimensions of the human being, the very idea of the human being, which the Nazis tried to remove from the world. As I have noted, the Nazis undertook an assault on humanity by undertaking an assault on the face, for it is precisely the face that harbors our humanity.

As they waged a war on humanity, so they waged a war on memory. But in these faces that live on and command us to choose life, memory abounds. Memory, too, lives on. Indeed, these lives are made of the dark memories that lie hidden within the light of life that now shines from these eyes. Yes, the eyes . . . You peer into those eyes, and you wonder, with fear and trembling, what have those eyes seen? That is where the memory is preserved—not in archives or museums, nor even in affidavits or testimonies, but in these eyes that have seen what we cannot fathom. You can almost see it. And you grow afraid. If death means oblivion, life means remembrance. Life means a never-ending return to life. And if these survivors and liberators could find the courage to remember and to return to life, we must find the courage to transmit that memory and to live on. "If we stop remembering," says Esther Loeb, "then six million Jews will have died in vain." Why? Because, Leonid Saharovici is convinced, "We can stop the hate by remembering." Still it is not only their deaths that must be remembered—it is their lives and the testimony to what is holy in life that their lives represented.

Somehow Robert Heller has taken hold of the memory in those eyes and laid bare a trace of what is hidden from us all. Having photographed a moment of tranquility in lives that have known a world-shattering upheaval, he has transmitted a silence that is deafening. The Nazis attempted to consign the Jewish people to a mass grave of silence, mute and empty of words and meaning. In these photographs, Heller presents us with a silence that is eloquent and overflowing with meaning. You look again, more closely this time, and suddenly you see what that silence is made of: it is the silence of mothers and fathers and children who cannot speak. It is the very idea of mothers and fathers and children that the Nazis tried to annihilate. The souls that ascended to the heavens on columns of smoke and ash now quietly abide here, in these eyes. Those souls, too, live on.

Coming before the souls in those eyes, we encounter our own souls, and we realize that the soul is made of the commandment to choose life, as they have chosen life, despite the kingdom of death that haunts them. We understand more profoundly the meaning of *Am Yisrael Chai!*—"The people of Israel live!" In these words there is as much summons as outcry. Where do the people of Israel live on? Not in the faceless masses but in every single Jew who chooses life, as these survivors have chosen life. We cannot comprehend the language of numbers so often associated with the Holocaust. We speak of the six million and understand nothing. But, thanks to Heller's portraits of the men and women who live on, we begin to have a sense of this one and this one and this one, each one somebody's mother or father, somebody's son or daughter, who might have been our own.

Anyone who studies the Holocaust is overwhelmed by a maddening frustration: we long to undo it. But we cannot. It is there, not only in our history but also in the very fabric of our being. We cannot get rid of the Holocaust any more than we can get rid of our own bodies. And yet something, in some small measure, can be done about it, as the faces in these portraits show us: we can live on, as witnesses to the fragile sanctity of every human life. "Can we eradicate evil?" asks Roman Mitelman. "I don't know, but we can sure work hard enough to try." That is what *Living On* is about.

DAVID PATTERSON
Bornblum Chair of Excellence in Judaic Studies
Director, Bornblum Judaic Studies Program
University of Memphis

NOTES

1. I say "European Christendom" in order to distinguish it from American Christendom. Although America has its Christian anti-Semites, the Jew hatred in Christian Europe was different from most Jew hatred in Christian America. For the Jews in Poland, for example, the two worst days of the year were Christmas and Easter, when Polish Catholics would hear sermons inciting hatred of the Jews as "Christ killers." At the instigation of their priests, the good Polish Christians would leave their places of worship to do violence to the Jews. Most American Christians have never heard a priest or a preacher declare to them quite so explicitly, "The Jews killed Jesus; now go out and beat up the Jews!"

2. Quoted in George L. Mosse, *Nazi Culture* (New York: Grosset & Dunlop, 1966), 316.

3. Immanuel Kant, *Conflict of the Faculties,* trans. Mary J. Gregor (New York: Abaris, 1979), 95.

4. See Ludwig Feuerbach, *The Essence of Christianity,* trans. George Eliot (New York: Harper & Row, 1957), 12–13.

5. See Friedrich Nietzsche, *The Gay Science,* trans. Walter Kaufmann (New York: Vintage Books, 1974), section 125.

6. See Hans Sluga, *Heidegger's Crisis: Philosophy and Politics in Nazi Germany* (Cambridge: Harvard University Press, 1993), 7.

7. Alfred Rosenberg, *Race and Race History and Other Essays,* ed. Robert Pais (New York: Harper & Row, 1974), 131–32.

8. See Eliyahu Kitov, *The Book of Our Heritage,* trans. Nathan Bluman (New York: Feldheim Publishers, 1973), 2:75–76.

9. See Louis Finkelstein, *Akiba: Scholar, Saint and Martyr* (New York: Atheneum, 1981), 103.

10. This term was introduced in and is used throughout David Rousett, *The Other Kingdom,* trans. Roman Gutherie (New York: Reynal & Hitchcock, 1947).

11. See Moshe Weissman, ed., *The Midrash Says* (Brooklyn: Bnay Yakov Publications, 1980), 4:423.

PHOTOGRAPHER'S NOTE

Photographer Margaret Bourke-White and author Erskine Caldwell titled their 1937 book on poverty in the American South *You Have Seen Their Faces*. When viewers look at my portraits, I want them to know that there is something powerful about these particular faces. *Living On* is a documentary project that includes photographic portraits of survivors, liberators, hidden children, and refugees from the Holocaust currently living in Tennessee. This group is unique, having lived through one of the most horrific experiences in history. They are witnesses to an event which, to this day, is still denied by some. Their stories, voices, and faces have been documented, and through this project they will live on.

It is sometimes said that if you look into someone's eyes long enough, you can see into that person's soul. Great portrait photographs accomplish this. Richard Avedon, Irving Penn, Diane Arbus, and Annie Leibovitz have influenced my work. As a photographer, a documentarian, and a Jew, I am drawn to the subject of the Holocaust from a number of different perspectives. It is my responsibility to make accurate and meaningful portraits, which will have value on their own and can also work as part of a larger effort that includes personal stories from the participants. These portraits and the stories accompanying them have never failed to elicit strong and emotional reactions from viewers. When one's photographs can be both visually powerful and emotionally moving, one is lucky, indeed.

Traveling the state of Tennessee for the *Living On* project, writer Dawn Smith, filmmaker Will Pedigo, and I knew that we were in for a moving experience. Listening to the stories of those who survived, who were hidden, who were displaced, or who were witnesses or liberators, we were constantly reminded of what an honor and privilege it was to hear their stories firsthand. As I looked through the viewfinder of my camera, I knew that the experiences of that tragic time were written on those faces.

Those who experienced the Holocaust will not always be available to tell their stories. It is the intent of the *Living On* project to continue telling these stories through both words and pictures so that the world will not forget.

Robert Heller
Associate Professor
School of Journalism and Electronic Media
University of Tennessee

Portraits of Tennessee
Survivors and Liberators

HERTA ADLER

Memphis, Tennessee
B. 1915, Diez, Germany
Refugee

"There are some people who say that Jews are human beings. Wrong. A Jew is a human like a flea is an animal!" Herta Adler remembers words like these from Nazi radio propaganda. "All the Nazi speeches encouraged people to look down upon the Jew and dehumanize him," she says. "People any time can be manipulated to hate and kill out of fear—fear that makes them not stand up against it—fear for any reason. It has to stop."

Because her father had served in the German military during World War I, Herta had permission to stay in public schools longer than other Jewish children: "It was lucky, I suppose, but just before I could graduate, I was asked to leave." At the next school, she says, "No one would talk to me because I was Jewish and they forced me to attend on Saturday, the Jewish Sabbath."

Herta was twenty-four on November 9, 1938, when *Kristallnacht* erupted: "One of my neighbors knocked frantically at our door yelling that the synagogue was burning. My heart began to bleed." She remembers that the Nazis closed a large orphanage for Jewish boys and "transported them to places unknown." The school's directors died in concentration camps.

Because Herta's brother did business in Portugal, where the government granted residency to family members, Herta and her parents were able to go there from Germany. From Portugal she went to the United States. "Since Portugal was more lenient with refugees," she says, "it was easy to get documents to go to America."

ETHEL BERGER

Chattanooga, Tennessee
B. 1902, Stanislawow, Poland
(Now Ivano-Frankivs'k, Ukraine)
Survivor: Stanislawow Ghetto

"We would walk for days and nights without food or water. We begged for help," recalls Ethel Berger sadly. "I saw my friend, my best friend, and she wouldn't let us in the door. She . . . shut it in our faces."

In 1941, Ethel, her husband, Herman, and their only son, Meyer, had been forced into the Stanislawow ghetto near their home. Ethel worked for German soldiers in a communal kitchen. "Nourishment was extremely poor; we were all very ill," she says. Occasionally she smuggled bread to her father, which could have cost her life.

Common to ghetto life were frequent roundups, called *Aktions,* in which Jews were randomly taken from their homes and killed. During one of these killing sprees, Ethel's father closed the front door to shield his wife. He was arrested and shot. Her mother, sent to a concentration camp, was gassed on arrival.

Ethel often thinks of her son, Meyer. He was thirteen years old, "wonderful and creative, strong and kind," she recalls. He hid during the day while his parents worked. "He wrote stories and recorded what was going on in the ghetto. He was a smart boy," she says. In 1943 Ethel and Herman smuggled their son out to live with a Christian family, planning to retrieve him when it was safe. "The Nazis caught him before we could reunite. They murdered him," she says.

Ethel and Herman left on foot, arriving in Soviet territory nearly two years later. World news told of Jewish liberation, but freedom was bittersweet. With Meyer tucked safely in their hearts, they began a new life in the aftermath of war with the birth of their daughter, Felicia.

MARK BLANK

Memphis, Tennessee
B. 1930, Vinnitsa, Ukraine
Survivor: Mogilev-Podolskiy Ghetto

"What I could never understand was [that] we had heard such awful things about the Germans and yet when they came to town, they were so generously welcomed by the Russians. How could that be?" asks Mark Blank, who grew up in Ukraine, which was then part of the Soviet Union.

When the Germans invaded in 1941, Mark's family tried to flee, traveling east via horse and buggy. His mother, suffering from tuberculosis, became gravely ill. They came back to put her in the hospital; she died soon after their return. The family home had been pilfered and turned into a cafeteria. Mark remembers, "We had everything gone. Some of our things were returned, but most were stolen."

They moved in with neighbors. Mark's father, an infectious-disease doctor, was given a special armband to wear. It allowed him to move about freely and to treat non-Jews. Mark recalls, "He was a great man and saved many lives. He treated everybody the same, without prejudice." Mark continues, "The Germans believed in humiliation. I remember they grabbed my grandfather by the beard and dragged him. When my father ran out to rescue him, the police began beating my father. This is not for a child to see."

About a month after the invasion, the Podolskiy ghetto was organized. A gate was built in the middle of the street. Mark says, "We had no right to leave. We had no rights period." They remained virtually imprisoned until the Russians reoccupied the city, liberating the Jews, in March 1944.

CLARK BLATTEIS

Memphis, Tennessee
B. 1932, Berlin, Germany
Refugee

"We were turned away and began sailing back and forth in the Miami harbor," recalls Clark Blatteis of his voyage on the ill-fated ocean liner *St. Louis*. "The U.S. Coast Guard wouldn't allow us to beach and eventually the ship returned to Germany."

Seven-year-old Clark and his parents were among the 937 refugees who sailed to Cuba in May 1939 to escape Nazi persecution. Following *Kristallnacht,* Clark's father had been arrested and taken to a concentration camp. His mother applied for permits to leave the country. Clark recalls, "My father was released from the camp to join us as we sailed out of Hamburg."

"The trip from Germany to Cuba lasted about two weeks," Clark says. When the *St. Louis* reached Havana on May 27, only twenty-eight of the Jewish refugees were allowed entry. The documents for all of the others, purchased from a corrupt consular official, were invalid.

The passengers stayed on the ship for five days. Then the *St. Louis* sailed slowly toward Miami. Telegrams to the White House and the United States State Department proved futile. The ship turned back. Belgium accepted 241 passengers, Clark and his parents among them. When the Germans invaded, they were trapped again. Clark recalls, "We ran and hid in our cellar and heard bombs going off overhead. After the destruction, we were arrested for being German nationals." Upon release, they traveled through France to Spain and boarded a boat for Morocco. After eight years in Casablanca, they finally made it to the United States.

OLGA BOROCHINA

Memphis, Tennessee
B. 1927, Mogilev-Podolskiy, Ukraine
Survivor: Mogilev-Podolskiy Ghetto

"In 1941, when Germany invaded, my mother, sister, and I were headed to Moscow," says Olga Borochina. When we reached the train station, we were not allowed to board." Within a week, Olga recalls, "everything changed. We had to wear Star of David patches on our clothing, post signs in front of our houses; we lost our jobs. We couldn't walk our own sidewalks or visit the grocery stores. Not even our Christian neighbors would talk to us anymore."

The rabbis prepared a welcome: "They brought the Germans bread and salt hoping they would be spared violence, but the Germans responded by shaving their beards and making them eat dirt." All of this came as a shock to Olga, who had experienced little anti-Semitism growing up in Ukraine. Olga's father, a physician in the Soviet army, was away on duty when their town was occupied.

The Germans created a ghetto by walling off a third of the city, forcing Jews to live in farm buildings. Olga says, "I lived there with my mother, sister, and grandparents in an open barn with goats. We had no walls and the snow would pile up inside. We burned anything we could find."

They lived there for three years. Her grandparents died from the cold. Olga recalls, "One day my sister and I heard that a mobile extermination squad was headed in our direction. We dug a hole and hid in it. We were there for three days." They were still in the hole when liberation came.

Today, Olga says, "It is hard for others to believe what we experienced. People do need to know. If nothing else, it might help them understand they can overcome anything."

WALLACE F. CARDEN

Clinton, Tennessee
B. 1924, Briceville, Tennessee
Survivor: Berga Slave Labor Camp

"I was hauling rock from one side to another. I looked up across the barbed wire and saw twenty-seven deer running by," recounts Wallace Carden. "I thought to myself, 'That's what freedom looks like.'"

Wallace was among the 350 American soldiers captured by the Germans during the Battle of the Bulge and sent from the Bad Orb prisoner-of-war camp to the Berga slave labor camp because they "looked" Jewish. For sixty-nine days they were tortured, starved, and ordered to dig tunnels through solid rock for an underground fuel depot.

Daily they got "an old slice of bread and a cup of watery soup." Wallace still has a pocketknife slipped to him by a sympathetic German. "When six of us had to break up the same tiny loaf of bread," he says, "someone always wound up cheated. Maybe he thought it was the only way he could help."

When the Nazis evacuated Berga, the prisoners were forced to march. "We walked for fifteen hours a day," Wallace remembers. "Some of us could barely stand. People just watched us as we moved through the towns. Some cried. Some just looked at us. It was as if they didn't know what to do." When the guards found a barn, he recalls, "we dropped right where we were standing and fell asleep." One morning, the Nazis were gone. "I ran outside the barn and looked up the road," he continues. "I saw American tanks coming and I began to run towards them. I kept falling down, I could barely make it but I got to our boys." Wallace had lost one hundred pounds in two months of captivity. Seventy of his fellow soldiers had died.

LEONARD CHILL

Chattanooga, Tennessee
B. 1932, Wilno, Poland (Now Vilnius, Lithuania)
Survivor: Wilno and Warsaw Ghettos

"I lost the ability to be too emotional," says Leonard Chill. "To this day I believe if you are too sensitive, you couldn't live with yourself for the horrible experiences of war."

In 1941 Leonard was nine years old. He and his father remained in Poland while his mother fled from France to Portugal to Canada.

Leonard and his father were forced into the Wilno ghetto. "There was tremendous overcrowding—four or five families to a room," he remembers. They escaped to Warsaw. "We changed our identities and took new names. I looked Polish so it was easier for me to pass. I was never in true hiding; I just hid my identity," says Leonard.

When the Germans began liquidating the area, Leonard recalls, "we knew we had to escape." His father, working on a road gang, detached himself from the group and fled on foot. Leonard, relying on his Polish appearance, walked away from the ghetto unnoticed. Father and son were briefly reunited before his father was captured and sent to the infamous Pawiak prison in Warsaw.

Leonard sold fruit and vegetables door to door. He remembers, "One of my customers knew I was alone and invited me to live with her. I never knew if she realized that I was Jewish." Six months later, his father was caught trying to escape and shot immediately. "I was ten and completely alone," he says.

A fellow prisoner with whom Leonard's father had entrusted details of Leonard's whereabouts found Leonard after liberation. Not long after, he was reunited with his mother. She was joyful and tearful, but he remained stoic, fearing tears would bring too much at once.

RACHEL GLIKSMAN CHOJNACKI

Nashville, Tennessee
B. 1926, Belchatow, Poland
Survivor: Lodz Ghetto; Auschwitz-Birkenau
Concentration Camp; Halbstadt Forced
Labor Camp; Salzheim and Freisig
Displaced Persons Camps

"I could speak German and I could work, my eyes were good," states Rachel Chojnacki. "I made little tiny parts for the ammunition; we had to make seven thousand per day to make the quota." Rachel was nervous when munitions factory supervisors came by and credits her eye for perfection with saving her life.

She recalls the most horrifying day of her life, when German and Polish soldiers came to take her father and older brothers away. Her mother instructed her to run after them, taking a backpack with a few belongings. As Rachel returned, she heard a shot. The next thing she saw was her mother dying in the street.

Rachel and one brother and sister were taken to the Lodz ghetto in 1942, where they were squeezed into a two-room apartment with ten to twelve others. Everyone worked from 6 A.M. to 6 P.M. at different factories. After about a year, both her siblings disappeared. In September 1944, says Rachel, "the people from our factory were taken together to the station." They were sent to Auschwitz-Birkenau for three months and then forwarded to Halbstadt, a forced labor camp in Czechoslovakia, to assemble munitions.

After liberation by Russian soldiers in the Spring of 1945, nineteen-year-old Rachel Gliksman made her way to the American zone in Germany. She found her childhood boyfriend and married him.

JACK COHEN

Memphis, Tennessee
B. 1932, Chalkis, Greece
Survivor

"On one hand, you cannot hold a grudge for the rest of your life; on the other hand, you cannot forget," admits Jack Cohen, who lived with his parents, brother, and grandmother in occupied Greece during World War II. He recalls, "I don't remember any anti-Semitism before the war started. We lived a very quiet, religious life."

In 1941, following the invasion of Greece by Germany and its allies, Jack's village was in the Italian-occupied zone. His family kept a low profile. His father kept them well informed, Jack recalls, "He spoke seven languages so he could translate radio news broadcasts and let us know what was going on."

In 1943 the Germans began arresting Greek Jews. Jack remembers, "Father contacted the underground resistance movement. They led us into the mountains during the night to safety." Greek Orthodox Archbishop Gregorios of Chalkis instructed monasteries and convents in the area to shelter any Jews who sought help. Jack's family hid in the monastery of St. George for nearly two years. When the Germans closed in, the family fled to a village in the forest. "My grandmother was captured there and we don't know what happened to her," Jack says, adding, "Townspeople reported that she was Jewish."

When the Germans pulled out, the family returned: his father to his ruined business, Jack to three years of missed schooling. Their home had been occupied by strangers. "Nothing felt the same again," Jack says. "I was quite bitter for a long time, especially about my grandmother. Eventually you just get on with the rest of your life, but you cannot imagine the loss—the pain. You just have to teach people about what happened. It is all you can do."

FRANCES CUTLER

Nashville, Tennessee
B. 1938, Paris, France
Hidden Child

"I remember most being jealous and resentful that I was not part of a family," says Frances Cutler. Growing up in various foster homes, she was often seated away from the host family's birth children, never sharing in the joys of dinner table laughter, toys, and treats. She longed for familiarity and security—and mostly for the mother she barely remembered.

Frances has had two religions, five names, seven homes, and eight families—all tools for survival for a hidden child during the Holocaust. The children (and their hosts) lived in constant danger. Many never saw their birth families again.

Frances's parents, Cyla and Shlomo, immigrated to France from Ciechanow, Poland, in 1936. Frances was born in Paris amid the turmoil of the German invasion. Worried that she could not protect her daughter, Cyla brought three-year-old "Fanny" to a Catholic children's home, where she could visit her weekly. Cyla was deported to Auschwitz in 1942, where she died, pregnant with Frances's only sibling. After that, Frances was taken to a Catholic farm to prevent her deportation. Shlomo joined the French Resistance and died from combat wounds in 1946.

In 1948 Frances came to live with her aunt and uncle in America. Even though she became an American citizen in 1953, her Polish roots and French upbringing made it difficult for her to feel at home anywhere. A trip to France in 1978 began the process of healing, although, she says, "it took a long time and a lot of work for me to let it go." She recently published a book in collaboration with other hidden children.

HENRIETTA DIAMENT

Memphis, Tennessee
B. 1918, Lodz, Poland
Survivor: Warsaw and Radom Ghettos;
Majdanek, Auschwitz, and Bergen-Belsen
Concentration Camps

"I do not have words to express the despair and horror of those years in the ghetto, but I remember so well how wonderful it was to be there at the uprising of the Jewish people," recalls Henrietta Diament. "We finally came to life."

During the Warsaw uprising in the spring of 1943, residents of the Warsaw ghetto resisted its liquidation for four months. Young Jewish men and women, poorly armed and facing a German force three times as large, made a desperate and valiant attempt to fight back.

When the Germans ordered Henrietta's parents into the Lodz ghetto, they sent their children to Warsaw to live with relatives. Henrietta's fiancé left his family to join her. They were married soon after and then forced into the Warsaw ghetto along with Henrietta's brother. Their father died of starvation in the Lodz ghetto; their mother perished in Auschwitz in 1944.

"What I remember most about living in the Warsaw ghetto was seeing children dead in the streets," Henrietta says. "I also remember being hungry. I was hungry all the time for years." But she never lost faith: "If I lost hope, I lost everything."

She and her husband were deported to Majdanek concentration camp and separated. She recalls going to Radom ghetto and says, "Then I was sent to Auschwitz, where I lived for over a month. One day we were stripped of our clothing and walked through the streets."

In November 1944, the camp was evacuated. "We marched all the way from Poland to Bergen-Belsen," she says. "My group was young and most of us made it." Liberation came in April 1945. Three weeks after Henrietta reunited with her sister in Belgium, her husband, Stéfan, showed up at her door.

RUTH DIAMOND

Memphis, Tennessee
B. 1926, Bialystok, Poland
Survivor: Blizyn-Majdanek
Concentration Camp

"It is too painful, too impossible to imagine what could be done to people . . . the torture, the humiliation, the starvation. It is just too much to imagine," says Ruth Diamond, who has never spoken about her Holocaust experiences before.

Ruth and her sister Helen were the only survivors of their family of six. The rest perished at Blizyn, a forced labor camp near Majdanek concentration camp. She says, "I lost my family that day. I lost them for nothing. It was Helen who kept me alive. Helen and I survived together. Helen was my sister . . . my best friend." Of her time in the camp, Ruth remembers, "I was working and that meant a bit more soup. I was with Helen, and we made airplane parts. It was okay. I had Helen." Their focus was survival. She says, "We didn't pray like some others did. I had nothing in the way of prayer. I just took it day by day."

As the war ended, Ruth and Helen were transported to two other camps, finally arriving at Bergen-Belsen, where they were liberated by British troops. Ruth says, "We couldn't believe it. I knew it was real when they opened the gates and we could walk through. We could finally eat again."

Two years later, Ruth recounts, "I met Karl, got married, and moved to Memphis to be near his family. I never even told him what happened to me and Helen. It was just too painful to speak of. He was also a survivor; he understood."

JAMES F. DORRIS JR.

Chattanooga, Tennessee
B. 1924, Chattanooga, Tennessee
Liberator: Dachau Concentration Camp

"We could see boxcars lined up with thousands of dead bodies," says James Dorris. "They just died right where they were stacked. We could smell the crematorium and knew the Germans were burning bodies. We began to realize what we were getting into. I saw inmates walking around and just staring at me. They were obviously confused and very weak. I had never seen what despair really looked like until that day."

On April 29, 1945, James and his army unit were sent to Dachau to investigate a "camp that might be there." Upon the troops' arrival, he recalls, "insanity was everywhere. As I met their blank stares and saw their starved bodies . . . it was more than I could take. I said to myself that this is what hell was like."

He was ordered to guard a fence separating the inmates from a moat until medical personnel and food could arrive. A fight broke out among the prisoners. Several were beating a man over something he picked up off the ground. Within a minute the beaten inmate called James over and gave him a rusty can holding a water-stained cigarette butt: "It was all he had in the world and he gave it to me as a thank-you gesture. . . . He had been saving it. My eyes filled up with tears."

James did not speak about his twenty-four hours in Dachau for many years. Today he is fueled by the need to educate others about injustice toward humanity for "no reason, no reason at all."

TRUDY NAUMANN DREYER

Knoxville, Tennessee
B. 1932, Unsleben, Germany
Refugee

"The rocks hitting the glass woke us up and of course I was terrified. Everything happened so fast, no sooner did the rocks come in than there was pounding at the door and my father was taken away."

Trudy Naumann was six years old on *Kristallnacht,* the "Night of Broken Glass," November 9, 1938. In her small town of Unsleben, Bavaria, Jewish homes and businesses were stoned and Jewish men arrested. Trudy remembers that night very well. She slept in the room with her grandmother, who suffered cuts on her feet from shattered windows just above her bed.

The Nuremberg laws had already forced her father and uncles to relinquish their profitable granary, but one relative who owned a winery saw his vines destroyed. Another, who suffered from mental instability, hanged himself in a hayloft. Trudy's father and other Jewish townsmen were kept in prison for a week. Fortunately, Nathan Naumann had already applied for passage to the United States, so he was let go. In mid-November the Naumann family departed by boat from Hamburg on the ocean liner *Orinoco.* Their saga did not end with the flight from Germany; they were made to wait in Cuba for eleven months until "sponsors" guaranteed them.

In 2000, Trudy and forty-three relatives returned to Unsleben. No Jews live there now. A plaque marks the former synagogue, the granary is now the town hall, the Jewish cemetery is well-kept. She relates, "People came up to us and asked us for forgiveness. . . . And they had a burden and we had a burden and we talked it out and there was closure."

SONJA DUBOIS

Knoxville, Tennessee
B. 1940, Rotterdam, The Netherlands
Hidden Child

"I never really felt connected to my foster parents. I don't remember feeling a part of their family," remembers Sonja Dubois. "I'm not sure why but I guess I just suspected something wasn't right."

Thousands of Jewish children were turned over to relative strangers by desperate parents in the hope that the children's lives would be spared. Many assumed new identities and never saw their parents again.

Clara Van Thyn was barely two years old when her Jewish parents boarded a train in Holland and left without her in 1942. It was a sacrifice that saved her life. Clara had been given to a friend to protect her from Nazi persecution and became a hidden child. Clara's parents were murdered in Auschwitz that same year.

A non-Jewish couple, unable to have children of their own, took Clara. Her name was changed to Sonja, and she lived as their child until the age of twelve. "When the family immigrated to the United States and I had to sign my passport, they told me what happened," she says. She was forbidden to discuss it, but Sonja refused to let it go. "I began reading a lot about the Holocaust. . . . My parents died when they were only twenty-nine years old. They let me go to rescue me."

"I did resent [that] I was adopted. I resented a lot of things, but now I don't," Sonja says. "My parents didn't stand a chance at that time and they knew it. They did the bravest thing on earth."

ROBERT EISENSTEIN

Nashville, Tennessee
B. 1917, Clinton, Iowa
U.S. Army Witness:
Dachau Concentration Camp

"We rode the jeep toward the barracks," Robert Eisenstein recalls. "People were still there. They looked at us. We looked at them. Hollow."

Bob shipped out in April 1943 as an officer in the U.S. Army. He was Jewish, but like the majority of American soldiers, he was completely unprepared for what he saw two years later at Dachau: "We got some vague information from periodicals, but nothing official. We never heard any rumors—nothing about what was really going on in Europe."

In May 1945, while headquartered at Fürstenfeldbruck airfield, Bob drove into Dachau accompanied by another soldier who spoke Yiddish. They were able to communicate with some inmates.

Bob says, "I can remember it clearly. All the houses in the town of Dachau had basements filled with different things. Some rooms had shoes, one had clothing, one had hair, and one had gold fillings." He remembers the cages in which guards kept vicious dogs that could be unleashed on inmates standing in line for food. He noticed that the German officers' quarters were neatly furnished: "I became sick, momentarily sick. How people could live so comfortably after doing these kinds of things to others. . . . It was all just too much."

Although Bob was in Dachau only four hours, the images from that visit are still vivid today. "I became most affected by what I had seen," he says. After returning home to Nashville, he realized that had it not been for an accident of geography, he and his family could have been among the Holocaust's victims.

JOSEPH EXELBIERD

Memphis, Tennessee
B. 1911, Tarnopol, Poland (Ukraine)
Refugee: Windsheim Displaced
Persons Camp

After the collapse of the Nazi regime, "oppressed people everywhere came out into the light again," recalls Joseph Exelbierd. "The lands they came from became graveyards to them. . . . They had nowhere to go." Exelbierd was one of only three survivors from an extended family of over one hundred.

Joseph remembers feeling disbelief and fear on September 1, 1939: "Poland was overrun by Germans from the west and Russians from the east. The borders were sealed and there was no escape." A math and physics teacher, he was able to trade tutoring for food and shelter at first. But in June 1941, Tarnopol was taken over by Russian soldiers and, he says, "the Jews were either murdered or forced into ghettos." He and his wife passed for non-Jews. They were put to work clearing land for train tracks and then transported to Kazakhstan in the Soviet Union. "Rachel and I were always together and that helped us survive," he says. "We suffered in leaving our families behind; we were cut off from everything and everybody."

In the spring of 1945, when Europe was liberated, an exodus of survivors traveled back into Germany and Poland. Joseph and Rachel Exelbierd came to the Windsheim displaced persons camp in Germany. In April 1947, Joseph was put in charge of the camp, becoming the first Jewish camp administrator in U.S.-occupied Bavaria. "We did our best to make this place a turning point—to create a process of healing," he says. "It was the only way to survive the pain."

HENRY FRIBOURG

Knoxville, Tennessee
B. 1929, Paris, France
Refugee

Henry Fribourg remembers "continuous streams of people walking on the highways to get away from German troops. People carried suitcases, bundles of clothing, knapsacks, babies; pushed wheelbarrows laden with grandmas or possessions; rode carts heaped high with household goods. Most were afraid of the German aerial bombardments they could hear from time to time."

Henry's father was drafted into the French army in 1940. Henry and his mother and sister were at their summer home in Fontainebleau. Friends lent his pregnant mother a car and their driver. Henry says, "We set out cross-country for Pau, a town near the border with Spain." Henry recalls walking alone one afternoon in search of a blacksmith to repair a hole in the car gas tank, but he attracted the attention of a German Messerschmitt pilot: "I was the only person in view, so I know I had his undivided attention as he strafed me with his machine guns." Henry threw himself in a ditch, but the pilot kept trying. "He missed me the first time, came around for a second pass and then a third," he recalls. "I must have really been a threat! An eleven-year-old solitary boy on a narrow rural road."

By June 1940, France had fallen. Paris was occupied by Nazi troops. Henry's father was allowed to rejoin his family in August, and after a few months, they moved to Algeria, a French colony. When Henry was expelled from school solely because he was Jewish, they escaped to Cuba, where they waited more than three years to enter the United States, finally arriving in Miami in April 1945. Henry finished high school in New York City. In 2004, he published his memoir, *I Gave You Life Twice: A Story of Survival, Dreams, Betrayals and Accomplishments.*

JACK FRIED

Manchester, Tennessee
B. 1938, Chorostkow, Poland
(Now Khorostkov, Ukraine)
Survivor: Chorostkow Ghetto;
Jablonica Forced Labor Camp

"My grandfather was hiding in an underground bunker during an air raid," remembers Jack Fried. "The guards found him there and shot him right where he was sitting. My father, uncle, and I went to look for him and found my grandfather dead, still holding his sister in his arms. . . . This is something you just don't forget."

In the ghetto, five-year-old Jack worked twelve hours a day with his mother and sister providing food for inmates and German guards. He knew that "taking food was punishable by death." His father, once a prominent businessman, labored at grave digging and road paving. He recalls, "It was very hard work and many did not survive it."

The family was transported to Jablonica, an agricultural camp in German-occupied Ukraine. His father and sister harvested food for German soldiers; Jack and his mother worked in the kitchen. "He didn't sit around and let things happen to us," Jack says of his father. "He fought and he saved us. My father escaped with my sister and returned home to unearth buried money he had hidden there." He bribed a German guard to smuggle Jack and his mother out and paid a Polish farmer to hide them all in his hayloft.

Six months later, as the Russian army pushed German troops west, Jack and his family traveled under their protection to Romania and then made their way through Bulgaria and Turkey into Palestine. Jack relates, "In Judaism we have a saying. It is *bashert.* It means 'meant to be,' and I believe much of our time after the camp was just that."

JAMES GARNER

Murfreesboro, Tennessee
B. 1917, Manchester, Tennessee
Liberator: Dachau Concentration Camp

"I had no idea what was happening to the Jews," recalls James Garner. "I knew there was a war, I knew about Hitler, but I really wasn't prepared for what I saw." Moving into Dachau in April 1945, James, an American soldier, saw bodies being put into crematoriums and burned: "The Nazis were just shoveling them in and setting them on fire." He recalls that some were even still alive: "Most of my troops broke down."

The end of World War II was a confusing, emotional time. American and British troops entering Germany met little resistance, and they came upon the concentration camps often by accident.

"Inhumanity, torture, starvation . . . it was everywhere. These were starving, crazed people," Garner says. Some fed the inmates, but he refused: "They were in such terrible shape. I didn't know what to do but somehow I knew I shouldn't feed them." Many who were given food by their liberators died; their stomachs, shrunken from starvation, ruptured.

"War brings terrible things to us all, but this was different," he says. "We came in so patriotic, so willing to fight. Then you see innocent people . . . abused and tortured—not for war crimes, for their religion . . . for their religion. Can you believe that? You wonder why you got there so late and who was responsible. You wonder if you did anything at all to help."

As James bows his head in tears, his wife Geraldine holds his hands and shakes her head. She tells him he did all he could have done.

JIMMY GENTRY

Franklin, Tennessee
B. 1925, Franklin, Tennessee
Liberator: Dachau Concentration Camp

"Off in the distance I saw boxcars lined up with hundreds of dead bodies inside. They looked starved and tortured," remembers Jimmy Gentry. "I asked another soldier, 'Who are these people?' He said, 'They are Jews.'"

American infantryman Jimmy Gentry had seen combat at the Battle of the Bulge, but it paled in comparison to what he saw that day: "No one told us what we would find. No one explained what our mission was. We saw a wall, and that was the entrance to a prison camp like I have never seen." The camp was Dachau.

They were told, "Get the guards and get out." Jimmy recalls his horror, "I couldn't move, and though I knew what I had to do, I was numb at the same time." He knew that soldiers died in war, "but non-soldiers? Just people? Religious people? I can't understand it. Not then, not now."

When Jimmy returned home, he was determined never to speak about it again: "I kept thinking if I didn't talk about it, it would go away." But it didn't, and in 1985 Jimmy met a Nashville survivor who convinced him to share his experiences with others. "Talking about it so many years later made such an impact on me," says Jimmy, who wrote a book called *An American Life* in 2002. "It was all too much. I was a young boy, a simple foot soldier moving from one day to the next. I just wanted to get away from that place, away from smelling death."

ZINA GONTOWNIK

Memphis, Tennessee
B. 1916, Lybeshuk, Poland
(Now Lybis Kiai, Lithuania)
Survivor: Wilno Ghetto; Kaiserwald, Stutthof,
Mühldorf-Dachau Concentration Camps;
Feldafing Displaced Persons Camp

"One day in the ghetto, the Nazis announced that all children were to be examined by German doctors," remembers Zina Gontownik. "I dressed my baby girl, Chaya, in her best clothes and hat. They wouldn't let us go with the children so I let my baby go, praying for a good medical report. It was the next day before we learned that the Nazis had thrown the children from trucks into ditches and set fire to them. Their screams were drowned out by music the Nazis played."

In the summer of 1943, Zina and her husband were separated. He was taken to a work camp near the front line with Russia. She and her sister were transported to Kaiserwald, in Latvia; to Stutthof, in Poland; and finally to Mühldorf, a subcamp of Dachau, in Germany.

Zina's husband and twenty-two other Jewish inmates escaped the Germans. He was captured by an advance guard from Russian army intelligence, which was investigating and monitoring Nazi troop movements. He fought with them for the remainder of the war.

Zina and her sister, liberated by the American army in April 1945, were transported to Feldafing, a displaced persons' camp in Germany. There a Jewish chaplain assisted them in getting in touch with family in Memphis, Tennessee. Through letters she learned that her husband and brother had survived. They were reunited two years later.

MATILDA STEINBERG GOODFRIEND

Athens, Tennessee
B. 1925, Teresva, Hungary
(Later Czechoslovakia, Now Ukraine)
Survivor: Mátészalka Ghetto; Geislingen
Munitions Factory; Auschwitz, Natzweiler-
Struthof, and Dachau Concentration Camps

"I was there long enough," says Matilda Goodfriend. "Long enough to see the misery and lose my parents and my brothers."

After Germany invaded Hungary in 1944, Matilda and her family were taken to the Mátészalka ghetto for a few weeks and then to Auschwitz. Transported again for work at an ammunition factory in Geislingen, Germany, Matilda stayed bound to her two sisters. "We took care of each other. With scraps of food or just faith, we held on to each other. We did it everyday. We survived the war together," she says.

One night as Allied troops closed in, the factory was bombed. Germany was losing the war and closing the camps, which pushed thousands of inmates into already impossible living conditions. On a train to Dachau, Matilda heard a voice pierce the darkness: "The Americans are coming." Tearfully she recalls, "The Americans were coming." Out of fear, the guards abandoned the train. Matilda remembers the chaos as prisoners delirious from starvation raided the food car.

After liberation, the sisters returned to Hungary. "But we came home to no one and nothing," according to Matilda. The family home stood empty, furnishings pilfered. No one else returned. They left their homeland and never went back.

Speaking often about the horrors of the Holocaust, Matilda says, "I pray that the children will hear me when I speak to them. That they will know and really hear me, so this never happens again. I pray that for them. . . . I pray that for all of us."

WILLIE HALL

Old Hickory, Tennessee
B. 1923, Livingston, Tennessee
Liberator: Nordhausen Concentration Camp

Just six days after his twentieth birthday, Willie Hall shipped out with the United States Army Signal Corps, bound for Europe. "We got word that there were some awful camps at Buchenwald and Nordhausen," he says, "but no one really suspected the death and torture of millions of Jews. How can anyone imagine that?"

His first memory upon arrival was seeing "sheds, several old sheds full of straw, dirt, and people . . . thousands of people, just skin and bones, stacked up in these old sheds." Willie remembers the condition of the inmates: "They were abused, tortured, starved . . . and the suffering . . . so much damn suffering."

When Nazi camp guards surrendered or were captured, American troops began asking inmates what they would like to do with them. "One said they wanted to make them crawl over the dead bodies that lay everywhere," he says, "so we did, we made every Nazi crawl on their hands and knees over the dead inmates."

Shortly afterward, Willie's unit shipped out of Nordhausen and headed for Buchenwald. "But I couldn't go. I refused to go," he recalls.

Willie returned to the United States in 1945 but didn't talk about the war or what he saw that day for over thirty years. "I couldn't even think about it. I had horrible nightmares . . . nightmares for a very long time."

HANNA HAMBURGER

Nashville, Tennessee
B. 1922, Eppingen, Germany
Refugee

"There were good people then, too. Not everyone believed what the Nazis told them," says Hanna Hamburger. "The nun at my school refused to allow me to be ridiculed. She protected me a lot."

Raised in Germany, Hanna Hamburger escaped Nazism at the age of sixteen. She and her family managed to leave just weeks before *Kristallnacht*. She recalls the fear and intimidation and the quiet exchanges between her parents. In 1933, Joseph Goebbels, minister of propaganda, urged Germans to boycott Jewish-owned businesses. The boycott bankrupted Hanna's father. Anti-Semitism was rampant. At Hanna's fifteenth birthday party, no one came. "I can still see myself all dressed up waiting for my guests," she recalls.

But she also remembers the Nazi physician who tenderly cared for her grandmother, the nun who protected her from anti-Semitism in school, and the German soldiers who urged her father to leave.

Hanna's father wrote to America and asked for a visa. His timing was good. When they arrived in New York in 1938, her distinguished father became a dishwasher, her mother a maid. Today, she admits, "I feel guilty for surviving when so many didn't. There was so much loss and so much torture."

JULIAN JOSEPH HOSNEDL

Clarksville, Tennessee
B. 1920, Prague, Czechoslovakia
Survivor: Klagenfurt Prison,
Dachau Concentration Camp

Survivor Julian Hosnedl shares an unusual perspective on the Holocaust: "We were all Czechs and we didn't like Germans because they were occupying our country and killing our people. . . . They even named our country Protektorat Bohemia and Moravia. Hitler had a very secret plan that they would move all Czechs to Patagonia in South America. . . . That was the reason we started working against Nazis."

Julian was an employee of Royal Dutch Shell when Germany invaded Czechoslovakia in 1939. When his boss, Mr. Sharp, disappeared, he realized something was happening to the Jews. Then the Germans began drafting young men into forced labor. They sent Julian to Klagenfurt, Austria, to stockpile warehoused food. He and five disgruntled coworkers began sending word of military activities to the Allies, leaving notes in a "dead box" near the border with Italy. In April 1944, they were put into a Gestapo prison with Jehovah's Witnesses and Austrian and Yugoslavian partisans.

Six months later, weak from hunger, Julian was taken to Dachau. Before he was deloused and interviewed, he watched forty thousand prisoners leave for work through the "Arbeit Macht Frei" gate. When asked his profession, Julian blurted out "cook" in hopes of finding his way to a kitchen. He was sent to cook at a remote ski lodge holding political prisoners. At war's end, he and others were able to aid a group of nearly starved, Hungarian Jewish women who had walked through the mountains from Ravensbrück concentration camp.

Julian returned to Prague. In 1968, when Russian tanks rolled into Prague, he fled Czechoslovakia for Canada.

FRED JARVIS

Bristol, Tennessee
B. 1935, Freiburg, Germany
Hidden Child; Survivor: Gurs and
Rivesaltes Concentration Camps

Fred Jarvis recalls being smuggled out of a French concentration camp in 1942, when he was seven years old: "My mother's courage saved my life. The fear of losing me to murder surpassed her fear of surrendering me to a total stranger."

His earliest memory is of the Gestapo coming to his home in 1940 and telling them to pack. Fred and his parents (his older brother had been on the last *Kindertransport* to England) and several hundred other Jews were shipped on cattle cars to Gurs, a French concentration camp near the Pyrenees, and then transferred a year later to nearby Rivesaltes. With the help of a cousin, they escaped, driving toward Switzerland to find the border closed.

As deportations to Auschwitz began, the OSE (Society for the Rescue of Jewish Children) surreptitiously collected the small children. Fred was given a new identity and taken to a farm. "Madame Burra was very good to me," Fred recalls, "She took me in as her supposed nephew at the risk of her own life." In school he had to speak French. "We had to learn very rapidly, without making the slightest mistake. Mistakes were fatal," he says.

At war's end, his brother Joseph located him through the Red Cross and found that their parents had perished at Auschwitz. An aunt in New York City sponsored Fred's immigration to America. He quips, "I spoke only French, lived in a household that spoke mainly German, and went to a school that spoke only English. I had a lot of adjusting to do."

NINA KATZ

Memphis, Tennessee
B. 1924, Sosnowiec, Poland
Survivor: Hannsdorf Forced Labor
Camp; Oberaltstadt Slave Labor Camp

"We had our own world in Poland but we weren't stupid. We knew who the Germans were. Their policies were not a shock. You learn to accept what you cannot understand. You ask why but there are no answers. I made it my mission to tell the world what happened to us and I haven't stopped yet. I keep that memory alive," says Nina Katz, who was fifteen when the Nazis invaded her country.

Growing up in Poland, Nina was used to anti-Semitism. She was not surprised by the German invasion or the subsequent persecution.

In 1939, Nina's parents, grandfather, and younger sister were taken to Auschwitz concentration camp. She says, "Because I was strong and tall and appeared able to handle hard work," she was sent to Hannsdorf in Czechoslovakia to work in a textile mill and then to Oberaltstadt, where there was a linen factory. She filled large spools of yarn on an assembly line: "I was tall and I could reach the machines so they kept me there." Nina recalls, "The older inmates who had been there the longest were mostly just confused. They kept asking the new arrivals what they had heard outside before coming in. Had they committed a crime? Had they done something wrong? Why were they there?"

Nina was among eight hundred survivors out of three thousand at Oberaltstadt. Her family gone, she married her childhood sweetheart and moved to Israel. In 1949, they came to the United States. To her horror, she says, "I arrived at the peak of segregation in America, and the familiarity was more than I could bear. I became immediately involved in equal rights among all people."

PAULA KELMAN

Memphis, Tennessee
B. 1927, Czestochowa, Poland
Survivor: Czestochowa Ghetto;
HASAG Munitions Factory/
Czestochowa Slave Labor Camp;
Bergen-Belsen Displaced Persons Camp

"I was twelve when my sister cut my long pigtails and applied rouge to my lips. I instantly became eighteen when the Nazis asked my age. It saved my life," says Paula Kelman.

When her parents and three of her siblings were sent to death camps, Paula remained in the Czestochowa ghetto with her sister and brother. She worked clearing out the homes of Jews who had been evacuated to camps and other ghettos and bringing everything to the Nazis.

Desperately hungry, she recalls how she wrapped herself in the sheets and linens: "I was able to take bedding and sell it outside the ghetto to buy bread." When she and another girl were caught, she remembers, "the policeman was Jewish and he shot a pistol in the air to pretend he had killed us, but at night he let us go." Another memory is of standing in the snow barefoot to watch Nazi guards shoot twenty boys as punishment for an alleged assault on an SS soldier.

By 1942, Paula was making bullet casings at a HASAG munitions factory twelve hours a day. "If we didn't meet the quota, we were taken to the back and beaten," she recounts. "When we looked at each other in the shower some of our bodies looked like road maps from the scarring."

At liberation, she says, "I remember seeing the Russians come in but nobody moved. We were so terrified that this wasn't real. When we realized we were safe, we immediately went home to find family." Their former neighbors turned on them, so Paula and her sister sought refuge at the Bergen-Belsen camp for displaced persons.

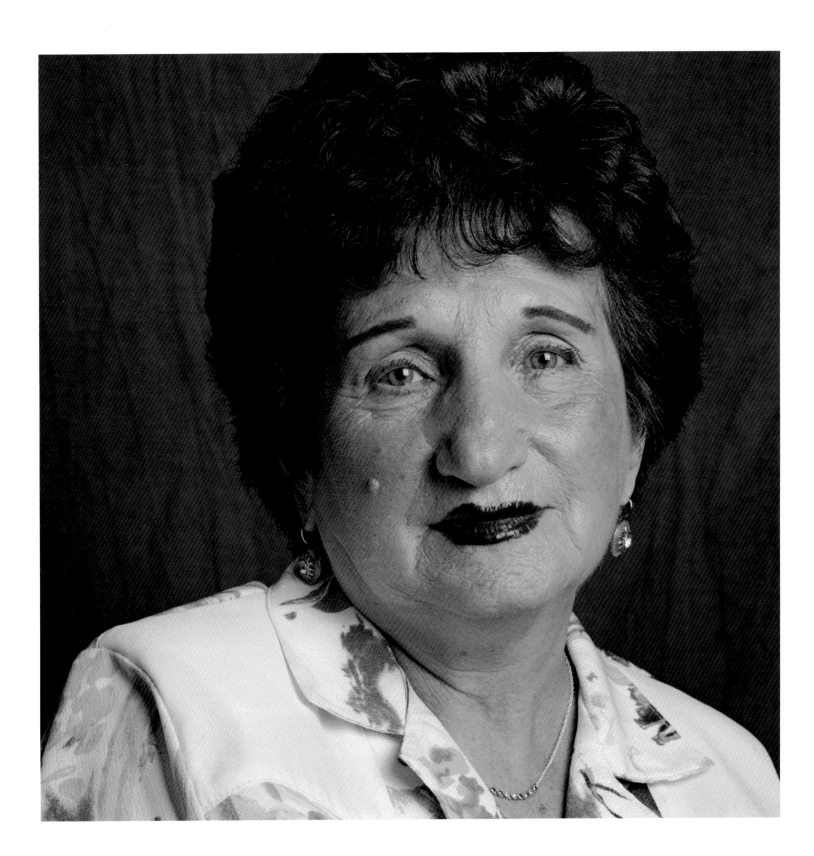

IDA FRANK KILSTEIN

Memphis, Tennessee
B. 1922, Oswieciem (Auschwitz), Poland
Survivor: Chzanow Ghetto; Neusaltz Labor
Camp; Bergen-Belsen Concentration Camp

Ida Frank Kilstein grew up with four siblings in the Polish town of Oswieciem, which would later become notorious as Auschwitz, the Nazi slave labor camp and mass-killing site established in May 1940. After the Nazis invaded Poland, the Frank family was forced into a ghetto in a nearby town. They were gradually dispersed. Ida was put to work in factories and moved from place to place. A final march away from the advancing Allied forces took her far into the heart of Germany, to Bergen-Belsen, where she and other prisoners were liberated in April 1945. Ida and one brother were all who survived of her family.

JACOB KILSTEIN

Memphis, Tennessee
B. 1915, Piotrków, Poland
Survivor: Piotrków Ghetto; Blizyn
Slave Labor Camp; Auschwitz and
Dachau Concentration Camps

"We would have to handle glass so hot, the skin on your hands would burn off the bones, and your back would break from the weight of what you were carrying." After the Nazis invaded Poland in 1939, Jacob Kilstein was forced to work in a glass factory and live in a ghetto.

The heavy labor weakened him. He was sent to Blizyn slave labor camp, where he was denied medical care and ordered back to work. He soon fell and broke his spine.

Put on a train for Auschwitz, Jacob somehow learned that his brother was on the same train: "On the train I tried desperately to find him. I looked every minute of that trip for him but never saw him until we arrived in Auschwitz. There were thousands of people around, but I found him. And then I lost him. And that was it."

By the time of liberation in April 1945, Jacob had been moved to the Dachau concentration camp. Freedom was bittersweet: "I don't think about that day like the others do. It is a painful reminder for me that no one was really free. Not when you have lost your family, your life, and all that you knew."

Still a hostage to such memories, Jacob is relieved by this quest for understanding what happened to the Jews. "It just tears at my heart that for many years, when we were willing to share, begging to talk, no one cared," he says. "I suppose I am glad they hear us now. But many died not having been heard. They deserved this time to speak—more than anyone else."

62

MIRA RYCZKE KIMMELMAN

Oak Ridge, Tennessee
B. 1923, Danzig (Gdansk), Poland
Survivor: Warsaw and Tomazów-
Mazowiecki Ghettos; Blizyn-Majdanek,
Auschwitz, Nordhausen, and Bergen-
Belsen Concentration Camps

"We boarded open coal cars, unable to leave, unable to move . . . for three weeks. We ate snow . . . there was no food. Fifty percent of us died in transport," says Mira Kimmelman, who survived a death march out of Auschwitz in the bitter winter of 1945. Under armed guard, she and other women walked for two days and two nights in sub-zero temperatures.

Mira doesn't know how she lost her family, but she knows why. When the Germans invaded Poland, she and eighteen members of her family were separated from their non-Jewish neighbors and forced to live in ghettos, where they suffered from hunger, extreme cold, and typhus. The Jewish administration of the ghettos opened secret schools. "To be caught with a pen or paper would mean instant death, so we taught privately through song and poetry. I was a student and then a teacher," recalls Mira.

In 1942, the Germans liquidated their ghetto and spoke of opportunities for work in the east. Mira says, "We believed it. Work meant security and food. We were hopeful . . . and we didn't have a choice. My mother and I were marched out of the ghetto toward the railroad station. An SS officer ordered me to step out."

Mira was sent to Blizyn, a concentration camp attached to Majdanek in Poland, and then to Auschwitz. She is haunted by a final memory of seeing her brother, who died at seventeen, at the gates of Auschwitz.

Mira's journey ended at Bergen-Belsen. With no work or food or water, the women drank urine to survive. In mid-April 1945 the camp was liberated by the British Army.

Mira is the author of *Echoes from the Holocaust: A Memoir* (1997) and *Life beyond the Holocaust: Memories and Realities* (2005). She says she finds her healing in "writing and telling my story."

WILLIAM KLEIN

Chattanooga, Tennessee
B. 1924, Ungvar, Czechoslovakia (Now Ukraine)
Survivor: Auschwitz and Mühldorf-Dachau
Concentration Camps

"It was so fast. They came in and all of a sudden everything changed," says William Klein, recalling the March 1944 arrival of German soldiers in his Carpathian mountain town. Nineteen-year-old William, a competitive soccer player, lost his job. His Orthodox parents lost their home. Most of the town's Jews were moved into a brick factory to await transport to Auschwitz concentration camp.

At Auschwitz, William was approached by a *Kapo* (labor foreman) who asked, "Do you want to live?" He replied, "Of course!" "Then volunteer to get out of here," the man said. William joined a forced labor battalion, bringing his twelve-year-old brother Sol along.

Assigned to ransack the abandoned Jewish ghetto in Warsaw, William says, "I was lucky. I went from house to house in a clean-up crew searching for valuables to be shipped back to Germany. When the SS wasn't looking we often helped ourselves to things we found. One day I discovered twenty gold coins. I traded one for two loaves of bread."

In January 1945, after a forced march to Dachau, William and Sol went to work at Mühldorf underground aircraft factory. When Allied troops advanced, prisoners were loaded onto railway cars. The train was bombed. The brothers escaped, hid in a ditch, and then walked into a farmyard. "The farmer was a good man. He gave us food and clothes and told us that the German Army had left and the Americans were coming." William remembers, "A captain in the American Army liberated us."

Back home, William located his sisters through the local police station. He traded a leather coat for their freedom.

YAKOV KREYMERMAN

Memphis, Tennessee
B. 1933, Mogilev-Podolskiy, Ukraine
Survivor: Chernovtsy Ghetto

"Nothing was ever the same without our parents. I never want anyone to experience what we experienced. To want peace in the world is not naïve. It is what we all want and we would know more than most what that means," states Yakov Kreymerman, who grew up in Ukraine.

Yakov was eight when German troops invaded his town. He had already lost his mother, and he understood little of what was happening. His father was sent away to the Soviet Army. His sister enlisted as an army nurse. Yakov and his younger brother went to Chernovtsy ghetto with their grandmother. It was bleak and frightening. He recalls, "For whatever reason, we were kicked out of my grandmother's house in the ghetto, and we had to live in a barn. What I remember about the ghetto is the hunger and cold. We survived on rotten vegetables."

"It was all so baffling," he says. "Germany attacked Russia, and all of the sudden Jews were the enemies. To our own! Russians everywhere turned against us. Like we were instant animals to loathe." Yakov learned the words "dirty Jew": "My neighbors and teachers called me that all the time."

In 1944, they heard that liberation was imminent: "A lot of people were killed on the last day because as the German soldiers moved out, they shot everyone they came upon in the ghetto." Many who had lived through the horrors of ghetto life died on the eve of freedom. Returning home, Yakov and his brother and sister found their house completely looted.

FRIDA LANDAU

Nashville, Tennessee
B. 1925, Pavlovice, Czechoslovakia
(Now Czech Republic)
Survivor: Auschwitz and Theresienstadt
Concentration Camps

"We were afraid every minute of our lives, and every day we had grass or even a sip of water, we were grateful. I guess we thought that was better than dying. . . . I suppose it was," says Frida Landau. She and her sister ate grass in an attempt to survive the ten-day train journey to Theresienstadt concentration camp.

By then it was 1945. They had managed to live through nine months of imprisonment in Block 16 at Auschwitz, where they had lost their parents along with their sister and her daughters. "It was during separation," she recalls. "We walked left to the showers and they went to the right. . . . They died never really knowing what was happening to any of us."

Concentration camp guards routinely separated family groups according to age and fitness to work. Teenagers and young adults were spared, while parents and younger siblings were often sent to their deaths.

At Auschwitz they slept four to a bunk. Frida remembers praying a lot and talking to others. "The Polish inmates had been there for about a year and would tell us many details," she says. "I could hear them but I just couldn't believe what they were saying. I knew but then I really didn't know anything."

Frida calls the day they were liberated in Theresienstadt a birthday. "[May 8,] 1945 was the birth of my freedom," she exclaims. It was a day she wasn't sure she would ever experience.

ELIZABETH LIMOR

Nashville, Tennessee
B. 1922, Lodz, Poland
Survivor: HASAG Munitions Factory/Skarzysko
Slave Labor Camp; HASAG Munitions Factory/
Czestochowa Slave Labor Camp;
Bergen-Belsen Displaced Persons Camp

"ARBEIT MACHT FREI" (Work Makes You Free) were the words wrought in iron on the heavy gates of the camp that imprisoned nineteen-year-old Elizabeth Limor.

Elizabeth worked twelve-hour days packing bullet casings on an assembly line in the HASAG ammunition factory in Skarzysko. At night she returned to grim, wooden barracks. She remembers, "The place was infested with lice and bed bugs. You could feel them crawling all over you." Once she and a group of other women were falsely accused of stealing a coat. Elizabeth was beaten with a rubber hose until she passed out. She wouldn't beg for mercy: "I promised myself I would never let the Germans hear me cry." But the women "cried together and tried to help each other. There was a lot of togetherness."

By January 1945, Elizabeth was at another HASAG factory in Czestochowa. Hearing that the Russian Army was coming to liberate them, Elizabeth and a group of friends, among them her future husband Irvin, opened "the tremendous iron gate." She relates, "We just walked out onto the street—we liberated ourselves." She was sent for medical care to Bergen-Belsen, a former concentration camp turned into a postwar displaced persons' camp.

From Germany, Elizabeth, her husband Irvin, and their baby son immigrated to Israel. Years later, after locating her brother in Tennessee, the Limors and their two sons came to join him. Elizabeth dictated her book, *Memoirs: Before, During, and After,* for her grandchildren. "When I finally wrote it all down, it freed my soul," she says.

MENACHEM LIMOR

Nashville, Tennessee
B. 1930, Czestochowa, Poland
Survivor: Czestochowa Ghetto; HASAG Munitions
Factory/Czestochowa Slave Labor Camp;
Buchenwald Concentration Camp

"Hundreds of people were crammed into these cattle cars. No food or water . . . we could barely sit. We melted snow to drink," recalls Menachem Limor, who was on the train for five days on his way to Buchenwald.

Snow offered survival. Menachem ate it and drank it and piled it up to stand on so he would appear taller to the Nazis who wanted to get rid of children too young for slave labor.

Menachem says of his childhood in Poland, "We were so close. I remember being very happy." After the Germans invaded Poland and shot his father, he says, "everything changed to the worst . . . the worst it would ever be."

His family moved into the ghetto in 1942. His mother and one brother were taken to the Treblinka death camp, but Menachem, small enough to hide in a hole in the attic, stayed behind with his brother Irvin. At a HASAG work camp, Menachem says, they met a "very religious man. He tried to teach the children whatever he knew. He taught us how to stay alive."

Two years later, on the way to Buchenwald, Menachem kept one piece of bread in his pocket for the trip: "Each night, I would eat one bite." On April 11, 1945, Buchenwald inmates climbed onto barracks rooftops to watch American tanks pull in. "They were coming from both sides," he recalls. "It was amazing." After liberation, Menachem was reunited with his brother Irvin. They have no family photographs. He still struggles to picture his mother: "I can't see her face in my mind. For me this is the most painful of all."

ESTHER LOEB

Nashville, Tennessee
B. 1924, Bydgoszcz, Poland
Survivor of a Siberian Forced Labor Camp

"Survivors were reborn through freedom. We have a commitment and promise to fulfill. If we stop remembering, then six million Jews will have died in vain," states Esther Loeb, whose family escaped to Russia from German-occupied Poland, only to be sent to Siberia.

Esther grew up near Danzig, where residents were bitterly split between German and Polish national identities. As she tells it, "They were always fighting each other, but they blamed the Jews for the civil unrest."

In 1939, following the Nazi invasion, Esther and her family fled east. At the Soviet border, small boats carried refugees across the river. Esther's family boarded, but her mother was pulled back. Esther continues, "My father begged to switch with her. He kept shouting to let him get off and let her go instead, but the boat pulled out leaving her behind." In Ukraine, they were robbed and had to go door to door begging for shelter. "Then," Esther recalls, "out of nowhere, my mother found us. Her legs were swollen from walking for miles in sub-zero temperatures." They lived in a barn for two weeks before the Russian Army found them and dispatched them to Siberia. Esther's father suddenly fell ill and died. Her pregnant mother gave birth to a boy who died of starvation before his first birthday.

In 1942, Polish civilian prisoners of war were granted permission to move freely within the Soviet Union. Esther and her sister sold stolen potatoes for train fare and took their mother to central Asia, where they found farm and factory work. At war's end, they returned to Poland, found no living family members, and then left to create new lives in the West.

HERMAN LOEWENSTEIN

Nashville, Tennessee
B. 1927, Hameln, Germany
Refugee

"The SA (Nazi Storm Troopers) came to our house and shot out the lights, threw milk cans through our windows. . . . We were terrified," recalls Herman Loewenstein. "All of a sudden we were no longer acceptable citizens."

It was known as *Kristallnacht,* the "Night of Broken Glass," and Herman remembers the nightmare well. On November 9 and 10, 1938, outbursts of violence, spearheaded by Nazi special police, occurred in German and Austrian towns and cities. Synagogues were ravaged and burned, Jewish-owned businesses were looted and their windows shattered, and Jewish men were beaten and arrested. Thirty thousand Jewish men were sent to detention camps.

Afterward, eleven-year-old Herman was not allowed to associate with his childhood friends. When Jewish children were forbidden to go to school in his hometown of Hessich-Oldendorf, Herman was sent to live with an uncle. In 1939, Herman left Germany through the *Kindertransport* program, an extraordinary rescue operation that transported ten thousand Jewish children to safe houses and foster families in Great Britain. He remembers, "I was sent to North Hampton. I can still hear the planes flying overhead." Herman was one of the fortunate ones; his parents came to retrieve him. They made their way to Montreal, to New York, and finally to Nashville.

At the end of the war, Herman remembers his father receiving requests for letters stating that certain officials in his hometown had never been Nazis. Those who once had turned him away now needed him. "Ironic, isn't it?" Herman muses. "They needed him now."

HEDY LUSTIG

Nashville, Tennessee
B. 1930, Höchst Im Odenwald, Germany
Refugee

"We were preparing to leave Germany," remembers Hedy Lustig. "We had papers to come to the United States. Then all of the sudden, we heard that the Nazis were planning to come in and rid the town of all the Jews. We couldn't imagine such a thing."

On November 9, 1938, when Hedy was nine years old, thousands of Jewish synagogues, businesses, and homes were damaged or destroyed. That night became known as *Kristallnacht,* or the "Night of Broken Glass," for the shattered store windows carpeting German streets.

Hedy and her family ran. "We stayed in the woods for several days," she remembers. "In November it was very cold and we were so hungry." Quietly, they returned to their home. Almost immediately, she says, "[the Nazis] arrived and took my father away. They beat him terribly, right in front of us, and they strangled to death the man who lived upstairs. It was at our dining room table. We were only children . . . to see such things!"

Hedy recalls, "My mother went to my uncle's house to seek refuge there. The Nazis knew everything, they knew where every Jew was, knew their families, and could almost always find them. They sent my mother a telegram demanding she come home to clean up their mess from the night they ransacked our home and took our father away."

Her brave mother went to the mayor, she says, and "for whatever reason—we may never really know— he told her my father was in Buchenwald and, hearing that he fought in World War I, arranged for him to come home." In early 1939, Hedy's reunited family came to America.

ROBERT MAMLIN

Nashville, Tennessee
B. 1924, Brooklyn, New York
Liberator: Dachau Concentration Camp

"I saw the look in their eyes as we arrived . . . those who had survived every hideous torture known to man. Their tears of joy and jubilation had finally been validated." Other memories haunt Robert Mamlin still: "Crematoriums . . . the smell of dead bodies. Half-buried women holding babies, their pitiful rags cast aside. They thought they were going to the showers and someone would launder their clothes . . . but they were gassed. They were just mothers holding their children in the showers. They had no idea."

Robert and his unit came into Dachau with other American troops serving under General George Patton in April 1945. Because he could speak Yiddish and some German, he was able to communicate with the inmates. Many told of the desperate final days at Dachau when the guards panicked and lost control as they learned that the Americans were advancing.

He remembers a young boy of fourteen who had lost his entire family: "By his brains and wit, he survived. He said he couldn't visualize that a Jewish soldier could actually enter the camps to help free Jewish inmates." The concept was equally overwhelming to Robert, whose military mission was also a personal one. He felt chosen, he says. "It gave me great satisfaction to be there as Jews were liberated."

NESSY MARKS

Knoxville, Tennessee
B. 1924, Pöszeiten, Lithuania
Survivor: Kovno Ghetto;
Hidden Child

"My five friends and I made a commitment to each other in the ghetto," says Nessy Marks. "Whoever survives must teach and tell the others. I am the only survivor, and I have kept my promise."

Lithuanian survivor Nessy Marks, her parents, and her four brothers were relocated to the Kovno ghetto after Nazis occupied their town in October 1938. What she remembers the most is betrayal by others: "Lithuanian Jews may have had a chance, but the locals—police, neighbors, it didn't matter—if you were Jewish, you were reported."

"It was also a loss of our humanity," recalls Nessy. "We walked in fear, wore stars on our clothes to identify us as though we were criminals. . . . Our heads were so confused. You knew you were not dead but you were literally not really alive." She thinks about the children in the ghetto: "They would come in and murder the children for one stupid, made-up reason or another. Every day you lived in fear."

Nessy's parents decided the only way to make sure she would survive was to place her in hiding: "I was slipped away and was hidden with a Catholic family for a few months. Rumors came to me that my parents were murdered, and I wanted to return to the ghetto but my foster family wouldn't let me."

Nessy answered an employment ad seeking domestic help. Fluent in German, she took the position but was warned by someone who guessed she was Jewish that bounty hunters were after her and would turn her in to the Nazis. Within days, she was offered safe transport to a farm in northern Germany, where she remained until liberation in 1945.

ROSE MARTON

Memphis, Tennessee
B. 1927, Chust, Czechoslovakia
(Now Ukraine)
Survivor: Chust Ghetto;
Auschwitz Concentration Camp

"After we were liquidated from the Chust ghetto, we were taken to Auschwitz," recalls Rose Marton. "The train was unbearable—no light, no water, no place to use the bathroom. We were like animals—that's why they called them cattle cars, I suppose."

Thirteen-year-old Rose saw her family for the last time. "I was crying and clinging to my mother, who tried to hold on to all three of the children," she recounts. "They ripped me from her, hit me over the head to make me move, and I let go of her."

Auschwitz was "hell on Earth," she says. "We were about five to a bunk. If anyone wanted to turn over, everyone had to turn over in order to move. In the middle of the night we had to stand outside for hours in the freezing cold, with no shoes on, so we could be counted. If anyone flinched, it meant a bullet to their head."

The SS called for seventy "beautiful girls for private secretarial work," she remembers. They were required to have "soft and clean hands." Fortunately, she says, "I had a rash on my hands and decided not to volunteer. I later heard that those women were used in a way that is shameful, and then we never saw them again. It is strange to think my infected hands saved my life."

Rose worked in an airplane factory near Hamburg, Germany, with four hundred other female inmates. Learning that the Russian Army was near, she and others left on foot. Scared and starving, they walked west for two days. "When we saw the Americans," she says, "we came out of hiding and felt safe for the first time in a very long time."

GEORGE MESSING

Knoxville, Tennessee
B. 1933, Budapest, Hungary
Survivor

"We realized this was not good and understood that we were being collected for worse things. As they marched us away single file, my brother and I slipped out of line and escaped," recalls George Messing.

When George was ten, his father was taken away by Hungarian authorities and forced to work at a military uniform factory. George's mother moved her young sons out of the city and found a job.

When Germany invaded Hungary the following March, George's father bribed a guard and got away: "He came to us and took my brother and me to a children's safe house that had a Swiss flag outside. We thought it neutral territory and we would be out of danger there. My mother went into hiding in a small town called Kiraly with her cousin. She gave us her address should we need it." A week later his father was taken to the Mauthausen concentration camp.

When ten-year-old George and his eight-year-old brother slipped away from the children's home, they went to their father's former place of business. Hungarian soldiers saw them there.

"They admired our escape," George recalls. "They said how smart we were and spared us." They took them to another children's home. "Several months later, the Nazis raided this shelter, too. We escaped again," says George. They searched for their mother. A sympathetic Hungarian soldier located her in the Budapest ghetto and brought her out.

They managed to rent an apartment where no one knew they were Jewish. "We lived on that fifth floor until it was over," George recalls. A year later, his father returned. He had walked two hundred miles. They left for Paris, France, and never looked back.

HELENE MESSING

Knoxville, Tennessee
B. 1934, Paris, France
Hidden Child

"We stayed at that farm until 1942," Helene Messing recalls. "Most of us were together. The younger siblings were at a home for infants, and my older brother was at a teen shelter. We could visit twice a year, which was nice." They never talked about the fact that they were Jewish: "No one could know."

Helene was five years old when she and her five brothers and sisters boarded a train to a secret destination. Their parents stayed in Paris, hoping the French government's relocation plan would keep their children safe. When Helene was eight, her parents, who missed the children desperately, sent for them to return to Paris. Soon after, on his way home from work, her father was arrested for being out past curfew. He died at the Auschwitz concentration camp.

Helene recalls, "After losing the children for so long, then learning my father had been killed, my mother had a nervous breakdown. She was taken to a psychiatric hospital. Our mother didn't recognize us anymore, she couldn't care for us; really, we were on our own. The younger ones don't even remember her."

The children returned to the French countryside and remained hidden until 1946. To avoid suspicion, they attended church every Sunday. Helene wrote to relatives asking for money to buy a Catholic rosary and communion book. She says, "My uncle read that and right away contacted a Jewish agency. They arranged for us to move to a shelter run by Orthodox Jews."

Helene met her future husband at a Jewish home for teens: "He spoke a little German, I spoke a little Yiddish, and we made it work."

ROMAN MITELMAN

Memphis, Tennessee
B. 1935, Minsk, Belarus
Refugee

"I look at my life before in many ways," says Roman Mitelman. "I had about a 98 percent chance of becoming a victim. If we are vigilant enough, we need to use our experiences to make sure nothing like this happens again. Can we eradicate evil? I don't know, but we can sure work hard enough to try."

At age six, Roman Mitelman began a struggle for survival. After Germany invaded the Soviet Union, his father had one hour to report for Soviet Army duty. He arranged for his pregnant wife and small son to go east. Roman recalls, "I understood that we were escaping the Germans but knew nothing more. No one spoke to the children about it." Minsk was occupied by German soldiers less than five days later.

The train was awful, Roman relates: "I remember the sign on the cattle car read, 'Capacity: 8 horses.' We were not eight horses. We were forty people, and we weren't even prisoners then—we were refugees. We had food because we used coupons for bread, but sanitation was a huge problem. There was no way to wash yourself or get clean water. We were treated like refugees in our own country. Our own country! We lived like strangers."

"My sister died, three weeks after she was born, from an infection," recounts Roman. "We lived on those cargo trains for three months. It was no way to live, and it was no place for a child . . . a baby at that." By November, he and his mother were in the Ukrainian village of Kugali. "Many had never met a Jewish person before. They were kind to us," he recalls.

His father was wounded on the Moscow front. His mother developed typhus. "My father came to take us to a better hospital in Moscow," remembers Roman. "[My mother] was very weak and sick, but wanted to see our hometown again. The sight of the devastated city tore her heart out. She died a few weeks later at the age of twenty-nine."

OLIVIA NEWMAN

Nashville, Tennessee
B. 1938, Vienna, Austria
Hidden Child

"Now listen, my child, I was always searching for God." Olivia Newman found these parting words in her mother's journal after she died. "Maybe she lost her faith? I don't know. She was always looking for some reason . . . something to explain all of this," says Olivia.

As a small child in Vienna, Olivia remembers kissing her father as he was being taken away. She never saw him again. She and her mother moved secretly to Hamburg, Germany, in 1941. They were no longer Austrian Jews; they were now German gentiles to anyone who asked.

"I don't remember practicing Judaism, but I do remember my mother lighting imaginary candles on Friday nights. She would also speak to her cousin in a different language, one I later learned was Yiddish." One December her mother placed a tiny Christmas tree on the table. The tree had eight candles on it, a symbolic reference to Chanukah, she believes.

It was not until the age of twenty-six that Olivia discovered that her father was Jewish and that he had perished in a concentration camp. She learned of her family's religious heritage from her mother's journal. Its old German script and cursive Hebrew writing revealed a history from which she had been protected.

"I suspect she left them for me," says Olivia. "I can't imagine what she must have gone through. Her imaginary ceremonies were signs of how much she missed that life. Ironically, without ever knowing it, I came to Judaism, never wanting to belong to anything else."

MAX NOTOWITZ

Memphis, Tennessee
B. 1927, Kolbuszowa, Poland
Survivor: Kolbuszowa Ghetto;
Pustkow Slave Labor Camp

**"The Germans posted proclamations that Jews must wear white armbands on their right arms,"
recalls Max Notowitz. "If you wore an armband, you could work on certain days. I volunteered to
work and proved I was a hard worker. It was one of the things that saved me."**

Thirteen-year-old Max was alone. His father was murdered at Auschwitz in 1941. His mother and two
siblings were killed after their ghetto was liquidated. He recounts, "They were unloaded from the train,
undressed, marched off into the trenches, and machine-gunned down."

In 1942 Max went to Pustkow, a slave labor camp near Krakow. He says, "Our job was to clear the forest: cut down trees and dig out stumps so the Nazis could build factories." Just as they were about to
be transported, probably to the death camp at Belzec, Max learned about a planned escape. "One man
asked me to go with them, and I agreed," he relates. They succeeded, hiding in surrounding forests
until Russians liberated the area in 1944.

Only then could Max begin to accept the loss of his entire family. "I was deprived of the gradual change
from childhood to teenager to adulthood," he muses. "I didn't exhibit any emotions during the war, but
it really came out after liberation when I realized how different my life was from others who had never
suffered." Eventually he moved to Warsaw and became secretary-treasurer for the American-German
Distribution Committee, a refugee relief agency.

Today, he says, "I have and gain a lot of strength from Judaism. In every way it is who I am."

REVA OKS

Memphis, Tennessee
B. 1917, Goworowo, Poland
Survivor of a Siberian Forced Labor Camp

"My father left one Friday morning to get Shabbat candles and didn't come back. He was rounded up with other Jews and locked into a synagogue. They were left there for hours and thought that they would be burned to death when the building was set on fire, but were finally released. I don't know why. There is so much about this that I just can't explain," ponders Reva Oks.

Reva grew up in a small town. In the summer of 1941, Nazi soldiers arrived and called all Jews out of their houses. Reva says, "They lined us up and forced us to stand for hours. My family was kept together on one side of the line." Miraculously, they were let go. They went to Bialystok and hid in a Yeshiva, a former religious school.

Her parents then sent Reva and her sister to Russia to scout for places to live. Reva recalls, "My older sister thought we would never be able to return to Poland and wanted to go back." Before they could return, Russian soldiers dispatched them to Siberia. Her parents and younger sister, living in a "safe" town near the Russian border, were shot and killed by Germans. In Siberia, Reva contracted malaria. She says, "We worked in a coal mine, and it was very hard work. There was no food, and it was bitter cold in the winter. We were sent into the surrounding forest to cut trees, which was worse."

At war's end, Reva and her sister wanted to return to Poland but found it impossible to do so. She met her future husband in Germany.

ARTHUR PAIS

Knoxville, Tennessee
B. 1927, Ukmerge, Lithuania
Survivor: Kovno Ghetto;
Dachau Concentration Camp

**"My sister carried my mother through the death march. [My mother] died one month after liberation. . . . We were very grateful to know that she was buried. What a thing to be grateful for,"
says Arthur Pais, who was among the 10 percent of Lithuanian Jewry to survive the Holocaust.**

Pushed into the Kovno ghetto after his town was destroyed, Arthur remembers, "German soldiers came in during a workday and took all the children and older people and shot them." Those who remained were loaded into boxcars. When the train stopped, Arthur's mother and sister were rerouted to Stutthof, a concentration camp in Poland. Arthur says of the last time he saw his mother, "My only memory of that day is of her crying." Arthur, his father, and his brother were sent to Dachau.

After working fifteen-hour shifts for weeks on end and surviving on watery soup and a daily slice of moldy bread, the inmates at Dachau heard rumors about the advance of the American Army. The Germans evacuated the camp, forcing the prisoners into a death march. Arthur's father, too weak to move on, stayed behind.

Starving, exhausted, and ill, Arthur and his brother pressed on toward the Bavarian Alps. When they awoke one May morning, they discovered that the guards had fled. They wandered to the nearest town. A few days later, American troops took them to Munich. It was there that Arthur found his father, just barely alive, and learned that his mother had at least lived long enough to see her home once again.

ROBERT RAY JR.

Nashville, Tennessee
B. 1920, Nashville, Tennessee
Liberator: Nordhausen Concentration Camp

"I will never forget April 11, 1945," says Robert Ray Jr. "I don't know that if I hadn't seen it myself, I would believe it. . . . I honestly can't tell you that. . . . It was just so, so horrible. But I can tell you . . . I may not have stayed very long in Nordhausen, but after what I saw . . . it was long enough."

Entering Nordhausen, Robert, an American soldier, thought it would be just another town. The Nazi guards had fled, and the Third Armored Division came upon a cold, dark compound. Electrified fencing surrounded what looked like military barracks. The soldiers used tanks to plow through the center of a wall.

Robert's first sight is one he will never forget: "Skeletons running towards us . . . crazed." Not sure what to do, he and the other troops gave up their only rations—and cigarettes. The prisoners didn't smoke them; they ate them, he says. "That's what starvation did to them."

Robert didn't write home about the four hours he spent at Nordhausen. In fact, he never spoke about it again, but he says that afternoon at the camp fueled his anger to win the war. Sixty years later, he can still see their faces.

ERIC ROSENFELD

Nashville, Tennessee
B. 1925, Seeheim, Germany
Refugee

"I asked him about my mother and what really happened to her. He told me he was ordered to send her and my uncle to Darmstadt." At that moment, for German-refugee-turned-American-soldier Eric Rosenfeld, time stood still: "I carried a pistol; the war was not over. I was in complete control. If I shot him, I would not be held accountable. What he had done to my family, to my childhood . . . all the pain and suffering I had experienced . . . it was unforgivable. All because we were Jews."

With emotions churning, Eric drove the mayor of his former hometown back to city hall. "Finally my head cleared and I realized I would not let him make me the animal he was," he says. "My heart tells me to take revenge, but my head tells me I cannot sink to his level."

In Germany in the late 1930s, Eric had seen schools and synagogues burned to the ground and businesses posting signs that said, "Jews bring us disaster" and "Jews perish." Eric and his mother appealed to the American Consulate for permission to enter the United States. He was assigned the number 22,000, but his mother's number was 33,000; this variance ultimately meant life or death.

Eric left Germany for New York, where he could live with relatives. In 1944, he joined the American Army. "Because I could speak German fluently," he says, "I was assigned to the counterintelligence corps and advanced with the 103rd Infantry Division into Germany in April 1945." Eric and other soldiers entered his hometown of Seeheim just before Germany's surrender.

EVA ROSENFELD

Nashville, Tennessee
B. 1927, Königsberg, Germany
(Now Kaliningrad, Russia)
Refugee

"Both of my uncles and grandparents had made it to the United States and were desperately trying to get us there with no success," Eva Rosenfeld says. When Eva's father fled to France on a fishing boat looking for a place to relocate his family, he left thirteen-year-old Eva behind. His decision made her both an orphan and a survivor.

In 1936, Eva was prohibited from attending public school, and her parents lost their right to work. They moved to Italy; her brother chose to stay and finish school. Eva recalls, "It was twenty-eight years before I saw him again."

Her mother died in Italy. When Italy allied with Germany, her father lost his business. After being jailed and released, he escaped to France to make arrangements to bring his family out of Nazi-occupied Europe. Eva stayed behind. When her father was captured and died in a concentration camp, she was orphaned at age thirteen.

Eva hid out with family friends until she was seventeen, living in various places with "very meager means. No running water or sanitation . . . lice, rats, and mice," and in "constant terror with German soldiers everywhere. It was never safe."

When the United States accepted 982 refugees from occupied Italy, Eva boarded an army ship with other "guests" of President Franklin Roosevelt. They were the only Jewish refugees allowed to enter the United States during wartime. Eva says, "I hardly ever spoke. I didn't realize it then, but I was totally traumatized by what happened to me." Eva completed high school, learned English, and graduated from nursing school: "At my graduation in December 1948, I was finally independent."

FRIDERICKA SAHAROVICI

Memphis, Tennessee
B. 1932, Targul Neamt, Romania
Survivor

"Every day another city was taken over. Our region, Moldova, was one of the last places where mass numbers of Jews were sent to camps. They just didn't get to us in time. It was always a matter of time," says Fridericka Saharovici, who can remember her parents listening to radio broadcasts beneath the bedclothes. It was a time of secrecy and fear.

Romania, allied with Nazi Germany, entered the war in June 1941. German troops flooded the country, adding muscle to the Romanian Iron Guard and its policy of persecution of the country's Jews. Fridericka's father and seventeen other Jewish community leaders were taken hostage. "They said if anyone left the city, these men would be shot," she recalls. Her mother took her to the schoolhouse. She could see her father through a crack in the wall. "The guards were so cruel. They said he would be shot and killed tonight." By the next morning the men had been sent to a forced labor camp.

In April 1944, as Soviet troops fought their way across the border into Romania, the Jews of Targul Neamt were marched away from the front. "We walked for several days. I remember the rabbi who refused a ride on a wagon. He believed that as long as the poor and sick would walk, he would walk." Fridericka says the battle over Moldova was "so fierce we could not return home until late September. Romanians stayed in our homes and helped themselves to whatever they wanted. Everything was looted and destroyed."

Fridericka finished high school after the war ended. She went to university in Bucharest, where she met her husband, Leonid.

LEONID SAHAROVICI

Memphis, Tennessee
B. 1927, Bucharest, Romania
Survivor

"Hitler killed the Jews because we did not have blond hair and blue eyes. We didn't fit the German notion of racial purity," states Leonid Saharovici, a founding member of the Tennessee Holocaust Commission. "We can stop the hate by remembering it and by never forgetting what the Holocaust was to many people. In Romania 420,000 Jews out of a population of 756,000 were murdered. We must teach about it and make people aware of how and why it happened."

In 1940, thirteen-year-old Leonid was expelled from school. His family's home was confiscated, their belongings put on the street. His father was sent to a forced labor camp. Leonid, his mother, and his grandparents moved in with his aunt—five people in one room.

Even before the formal alliance with Nazi Germany in June 1941, Romania's Iron Guard enforced racial hatred: "People were put out of business and dismissed from jobs." Leonid calls it anarchy; no rule of law could protect the Jews. In one vicious raid, Leonid recalls, Jews were "taken and placed in slaughterhouses. The fascist militia ran out of ammunition, so they put Jews on meat hooks."

Leonid went daily to a forced labor camp. "We did everything we were asked," he recalls. "Much was not so pleasant for a boy of fifteen." One very cold day, when Leonid was shoveling snow, a kind woman appeared. "She called to us and offered us hot tea and some bread," he says. "Her husband came home and began yelling, 'What are you doing? These are dirty Jews, let them freeze . . . they must die.' She pushed him into the house, told us to finish the tea and leave. Her heart was in the right place."

RAYMOND SANDVIG

Hermitage, Tennessee
B. 1920, Sioux Falls, South Dakota
Military Liaison: Nuremberg War Crimes Trials

"I worked up a plan so they could attend and realize this was serious and we weren't just there for revenge or show," says Ray Sandvig, an American army officer involved in the Nuremberg Trials. He adds that it was "very important to me to let the Germans believe in what we were doing."

The Nuremberg Trials were convened by the Allied powers to sit in judgment on those suspected of crimes against humanity during World War II. When Ray thinks back, he is overwhelmed. "I remember one day just sitting at my desk and tears came running down my cheek," he says. "It was just too much, you know, too much hitting the body all at once. It was part of history, a time for retribution. A very important time for many."

Ray was surprised to see how many German civilians supported the process. Many were quick to denounce Nazism—a protest that could have cost them their lives just months before.

He recalls the "doctors' trial" for those who performed medical testing and experimentation on Jewish prisoners. He heard a witness describe how German physicians froze fully conscious live subjects in an experiment to determine the limits the human body could withstand. The victims often died or were permanently disfigured.

Twenty-two "major" German and Austrian war criminals were tried during eleven months of hearings at Nuremberg. Other tribunals throughout Europe would continue the work begun at Nuremberg, and a number of low-level officials were convicted, but many Nazis and Nazi collaborators were never brought to justice.

ALEXANDER SAVRANSKIY

Memphis, Tennessee
B. 1930, Tomashpol, Ukraine
Survivor: Tomashpol Ghetto

"They hated us, they prepared for our deaths . . . but why?" Alexander Savranskiy still wonders why the Jewish people were targeted for extermination by the Nazis. "I don't know. I was never really the same. How could a boy be changed so deeply, so permanently? I was."

Alexander's hometown was occupied by German soldiers after Russia was invaded. When his father became sick with a high fever, they learned that prescriptions were forbidden to Jews. "My mother and grandmother tried to help by wrapping him in linens," remembers Alexander, "but since we were not allowed to have medicine or even buy it, we could not save him."

After his father died, his mother moved to nearby Vinnitsa to earn a living for the family. Eleven-year-old Alexander and his grandmother were sent to the Tomashpol ghetto. His cousins were rounded up to go to work; instead they were shot to death, and their bodies fell into a common grave.

When the Soviet Army retook the town three years later, he recalls, "we heard the shooting first but we never believed the Russians could win. It was strange. Even though they liberated us, they were hateful to us. They rescued us but called us 'dirty Jews' the whole time."

At war's end, Alexander and his mother stayed in Vinnitsa for several years while he tried to catch up in school. Even now, he says, "you can still see the sadness in the Jewish eyes. When I can't sleep at night now, it is always because of that. I see them still."

GERTRUDE SCHLANGER

Nashville, Tennessee
B. 1925, Sobrance, Czechoslovakia
(Now Slovakia)
Survivor: Auschwitz Concentration Camp

"Eat whatever they feed you . . . please. . . . You need it so you will survive." These were the parting words of a father to his three daughters, spoken through a fence dividing parents from children. "It was at separation," Gertrude Schlanger recalls. "You were moved into different lines but you just didn't know that would be the last time you would see each other. You could have said goodbye; instead, you looked at each other . . . terrified . . . and then it was over."

Gertrude and her sisters spent the winter of 1945 in Auschwitz hauling potatoes in the bitter cold. As rumors circulated about possible liberation by the Russian army, Gertrude and twenty-two others decided to try to escape. On a forced march from a camp she can barely recall, she says, "we were put in haystacks to sleep. We hid beneath the hay and when the guard called on us to start walking, we stayed behind in the straw." No one noticed as the women fled the next day. Gertrude and her sisters boarded a train. "We had heard the Russians had come in, and I guess we thought we could safely ride a train. No money, no food, barely any clothes. . . . I suppose we just didn't care anymore." No one asked them for train fare.

Because they were among the first Jews to return to Czechoslovakia, they were able to retrieve their home and its furnishings from their neighbors. Gertrude muses, "People have told me they think I just tell stories about what happened. . . . They didn't lose their whole family in a line. . . . They have no idea what pain is."

RALPH SCHULZ

Nashville, Tennessee
B. 1926, Alton, Illinois
Special Services Officer:
Nuremberg War Crimes Trials

"Good Germans are being put to death in gas chambers," read a headline in a Catholic periodical in 1945. Ralph Schulz recalls this news bulletin as the first he had heard of the atrocities against the Jews.

Because he could speak German, infantryman Ralph Schulz was sent to Germany in 1945 to assist U.S. Army lawyers with the Nuremberg Trials. "My job overseas was to provide documents and evidence for the trials and particularly those being tried," he says. He spoke to many survivors, and he was present during Hermann Göring's trial.

Göring, a senior Nazi official, had been responsible for giving the order to carry out the Final Solution, the plan for the total destruction of the Jews in Europe. Ralph recalls that Göring was delusional and thought the judge "and everyone there would just snap to attention, follow his orders, and accept his testimony." Ralph says, "He genuinely believed he had served the German people with honor." Although he knows the survivors suffered at hearing Göring's testimony, Ralph says that "there was healing for them, too . . . at being present as he was brought to justice." He continues, "Göring wasn't right. He was grasping for a rationale. Many were. But, it was a time for justice." Göring was found guilty on all counts but committed suicide in prison just hours before his scheduled hanging.

"The job was tough emotionally," Ralph remembers. As he returned to the United States in March 1947, he carried the weight of all he had seen and heard at Nuremberg with him.

JACK SEIDNER

Nashville, Tennessee
B. 1921, Lujan, Romania (Now Ukraine)
Survivor: Transniester Labor Camp

"I lost a lot of my life for nothing, but we made it and we're here," says Jack Seidner. His ordeal began in 1941 and didn't end until he made it to Nashville in 1954.

Jack grew up in the Bukovina region, in formerly Austrian Romania. Lujan, a small farm town, had two synagogues and a hundred Jewish families. In 1940, they found themselves caught between Romanian Iron Guard troops and unsympathetic Ukrainian neighbors. He and others were sent to the Transniester, a contested border region, to work on the railroad under German and Ukrainian guard. When they returned, their homes had been emptied. They were held in a sugar factory, then force-marched north into Poland. The elderly rode in buggies. "I put my mother in one and my father in another," Jack recalls, "and the young people had to march in front, and we got there in the morning and the only people who disappeared that night were my father and mother and another couple. What happened to them that night I will never know; they must have killed them."

After three months' march, only three hundred were left from an original group of fifteen hundred. Jack worked at hard labor in Poland until the end of 1944, when he was put on a train headed for a concentration camp in Germany. Russian airplanes bombed the train, and the prisoners ran into the woods and escaped. At war's end, hoping to immigrate to Palestine, Jack found his way to a Jewish agricultural training facility near Bucharest. It was there that he met his future wife, Sara Slomovic, and her sister Lea.

ERIKA SIGEL

Memphis, Tennessee
B. 1927, Bardejov, Czechoslovakia
(Now Slovakia)
Hidden Child

"As a child I had a best friend who wasn't Jewish," recalls Erika Sigel. "I was like a member of her family until Hitler came into power with all his lies. They shut the door on me and our relationship forever after that."

At first Erika's father was granted special permission to stay in Czechoslovakia because he was a grocer, and, as she puts it, "The town needed him." One of her brothers found her a live-in job as a housekeeper with a family who was willing to keep her Judaism a secret. Erika took the Jewish star off her clothing so she could buy food at the market. "There was one gentile girl who knew I was Jewish but she never gave me away," she says. "I got to feel normal for a few minutes at a time."

Then her mother and her four brothers were sent to Auschwitz. Sorrowfully she says, "I had no contact with them at all before they left." Her father was taken away soon afterward. The family she stayed with treated her decently. German soldiers occupying the town moved into the house where she had been raised. She says of those days, "I pretended not to understand German so the soldiers couldn't figure out I was Jewish. I had to have a poker face. I couldn't laugh or cry or even look their way. I was always on guard."

When the Russian Army liberated the town, Erika volunteered to work in a soup kitchen for those returning from concentration camps. She says, "I worked for free hoping to see some of my family come back." One of her brothers arrived at the kitchen, and they went to Belgium to secure a visa for travel to the United States.

Erika laments, "Of my four brothers, three came back. My parents and youngest brother died in Auschwitz. It was a horrible, horrible time, but I was grateful to the family that kept me alive." Erika remains in touch with the family who gave her refuge. She sends them a gift of money every year.

ELLA SILBER

Memphis, Tennessee
B. 1924, Jonava, Lithuania
Survivor: Stutthof and Dachau
Concentration Camps

"We had heard some gossip about the Germans but back then," says Ella Silber, "if you didn't see it, you didn't really believe it. I mean who could believe such things?"

In 1940, Ella Silber's hometown in Lithuania was taken over by Russians. A year later, Germans arrived and forced Ella, her mother, and her three brothers into a ghetto. "We had to share a house with another family and wore yellow Stars of David on our clothing," she says. "I worked all day long doing hard, manual labor, but I was young. Young enough to withstand it, I suppose."

Three years later, Ella was sent to a concentration camp. She never saw her family again. "They were all killed in the ghetto," she says. "In the last days of the war, we were thrown out of our barracks and forced to begin a death march," she recalls, and when leaving Dachau, "we were given a piece of bread and a tin of soup for the journey."

As American troops advanced, thousands of prisoners stumbled south in the freezing cold. German guards shot anyone who could no longer continue. Ella awoke one day to find the guards gone.

At an American-run displaced persons' camp, Ella met the man she would marry and was reunited with her second cousin, who was an American soldier. As she tells it, "He returned looking for relatives and found only me." She continues, "I can't understand why the Holocaust happened, I just know I don't like to talk about it. Make no mistake. I remember everything, but it is very hard to talk about it."

LEA SLOMOVIC NAFT

Nashville, Tennessee
B. 1926, Kolockawa, Czechoslovakia
Survivor: Sekernice Ghetto; Stutthof Slave Labor
Camp; Auschwitz Concentration Camp

SARA SLOMOVIC SEIDNER

Nashville, Tennessee
B. 1927, Kolockawa, Czechoslovakia
Survivor: Sekernice Ghetto; Stutthof Slave Labor
Camp; Auschwitz Concentration Camp

"When the Hungarians came in, in 1939, the trouble started then," says Lea Naft. "We didn't know what was going on. We didn't have radios. We were standing by the window. 'Look, it's different soldiers,' we said. The Germans had gray uniforms. They marched in and started working together with the Hungarians."

Lea and her sister Sara Slomovic grew up in a small town in Czechoslovakia's Carpathian mountains. There were only fifty to sixty families, mostly Christians. Because of their self-sufficiency as a farm family, the Slomovic family kept to themselves during the first years of Nazi domination. In 1941, they were put under house arrest, made to wear yellow stars, and no longer allowed in the streets. Officials ordered every family out for questioning and then released them after twenty-four hours. They heard rumors about people being taken to ghettos and one day even saw a line of Jews marching through from another town. The soldiers came for them at the end of 1942, Lea recalls, and "they said, 'Get your belongings, you have to go.'"

The two sisters managed to stay together as they were moved from ghetto to labor camp to concentration camp. At one point on a long march, Lea became so sick that she couldn't eat. Sara and a friend half-carried her through the snow. Finally liberated by Allied soldiers at Putzk, Lea recalls that Sara somehow found a goose, made soup, and nursed her back to health. Today Sara is no longer able to cook, so it is Lea who prepares the weekly family meal.

HARRY SNODGRASS

Mt. Juliet, Tennessee
B. 1922, Johnson City, Tennessee
Liberator: Buchenwald Concentration Camp

"Inmates everywhere," Harry Snodgrass remembers. "Some dead and some alive under the dead . . . just lying there. I couldn't think. No thoughts came to my head. Only horror. I had never seen anything like this before."

As they drove into the Buchenwald concentration camp in April 1945, Harry recalls a fellow American soldier saying to him, "There isn't a God in heaven . . . no God at all."

He toured the camp with a Lithuanian inmate who spoke broken English. Harry's voice trails off as he recalls the memories: "It was in the commander's office. There were lampshades made from the skin of Jews. In the crematorium they used the ashes of the inmates to fertilize the fields—the ashes of dead people. After an hour, it just became too much. I was stunned . . . just stunned. We don't even treat dogs like this."

Harry and the other soldier retreated and moved on to Berlin as ordered. For Harry, the hour at Buchenwald became six decades of nightmares. He had enlisted in the army at age twenty, and although he knew of the hatred the Germans had for the Jews, he was shocked at the atrocities. With pain evident in his eyes, Harry struggles with the complacency of the local townspeople living near the camp: "They saw the trains going in, but no one saw them leave. If they say they didn't know what was happening, they were lying."

Today Harry Snodgrass speaks to schools and gatherings about what he saw as a liberator. He stresses the danger of racial and religious divisiveness: "I tell them what I have known all my life. . . . For evil to exist it just takes good people to do nothing."

PAULA STEIN

Memphis, Tennessee
B. 1926, Bendzin, Poland
Survivor: Bendzin Ghetto;
Mauthausen Concentration Camp

"When it became too much at the camp, I would dream. I would dream about *Shabbos*, about my mother baking *challah*, my father saying the prayers. . . . I could not have survived without pretending even for a few moments that I was anywhere but here in this hell," recounts Paula Stein.

In September 1939, German soldiers forced Paula's family and other building residents into the back-yard. "My father put his prayer shawl under his coat in case he would need to pray," she remembers. The soldiers lined women up on one side and men on the other. "My father and brother were shot right in front of us," says Paula. "I was holding my younger sister at the time. My mother could not move."

They spent the night in her uncle's cellar. The next day, her mother insisted on returning to bury the dead. "We carried their bodies ourselves and dug their graves with our hands," Paula recalls. They were sent to the ghetto: "We were cold and we were hungry, but the truth is nothing could hurt us after what we had just seen."

In 1943, her mother, grandmother, and sister were put on a train to Auschwitz. Paula's train went to Mauthausen, where girls lived twenty-four to a room. In March 1945, they were marched away to prevent their capture by the Allies. She and another girl fled and were freed by the Soviet army on May 5. Paula sought information on relatives at displaced persons' camps. In 1948, at a displaced persons' camp in Italy, she met and married Sol. Her aunt helped bring them to Memphis.

SOL STEIN

Memphis, Tennessee
B. 1920, Slobodka, Lithuania
Survivor: Kovno Ghetto;
Dachau Concentration Camp

"What I remember most about the Lithuanians was the betrayal," says Sol Stein. "We had a neighbor who we fed and cared for regularly, but when the Germans moved in, he turned us in to them. Just like that. We went from feeding and helping him to hiding from him."

After the German invasion in 1941, anti-Semitism spread. Sol's mother fled to Russia, leaving her five children behind. The Germans forced Sol and his four sisters into the Kovno ghetto. Digging ditches kept him alive: "I was always used to hard work. I think the hard work of the ghetto kept me moving, kept me clearheaded."

Sol was later transported to Dachau in a railcar crammed with a hundred people. His job at the camp was loading bags of cement. He says, "There was a guard who used to give me a piece of bread. I don't know why. He was kind I guess." Once he was caught praying: "A guard saw us. He knew what we were doing so he took us outside. In the freezing weather he sprayed ice water on us. It was so cold, but we would have done it again."

In 1945, as the American army advanced, the Germans evacuated. Sol recalls, "They told us they were marching us from Dachau to Switzerland, so we walked. We walked for weeks in the freezing cold. More than half of us died along the way." He describes coming upon a dead horse: "We went crazy, ripping it to pieces and eating it. In less than a few minutes there was nothing left of that horse." At war's end, Sol weighed no more than seventy pounds.

HANS STRUPP

Nashville, Tennessee
B. 1921, Frankfurt, Germany
Refugee

**"Some got out and some didn't. We were lucky that our family sponsorship arrived in time,"
recalls Hans Strupp, who counts himself very fortunate to have come to the United States
in 1939.**

Hans's American uncle completed the affidavit required for immigration to the United States, promising
financial support so that Hans and his mother and brother could leave Germany. He remembers every
difficult day leading up to their departure. The Nuremberg laws passed in 1935 legally excluded Jews
from German life and became the foundation for further anti-Jewish policies. Every element of life was
upended, from public schools to employment, shopping, and entertainment. Some childhood friends
no longer came around. Hans recalls, "We were human and then we weren't. It happened so quickly,
and yet it was probably always there."

Hans and his family left for the United States. Their furniture, photo albums, household goods, and clothing were neatly packed, but they never arrived. "We were Jews. We weren't allowed the luxuries of even
our own clothing."

Hans has never forgotten what might have been: "We knew we were lucky. We always knew. No one
could anticipate what was to happen. Rumors, even at their worst, never revealed such a nightmare."

RAISA TERK (KREYMERMAN)

Memphis, Tennessee
B. 1936, Mogilev, Ukraine
Refugee

Raisa Terk (the wife of Yakov Kreymerman) was only a child when her father was called into the Russian army. During the Nazi occupation, she fled with her mother and brother to Magnitogorsk. Her grandparents were pushed into the Mogilev ghetto and later perished at Mogilev-Podolskiy concentration camp. At war's end, her father came home, and the family was able to return to Mogilev.

SIMON WAKSBERG

Memphis, Tennessee
B. 1921, Lodz, Poland
Survivor: Lodz Ghetto; Poznan and
Andrzejewo Forced Labor Camps;
Auschwitz and Flossenburg
Concentration Camps

"Do not hate; hate will eat you up. Remember the past but live for the future," says Simon Waksberg, who likes to speak to teenagers.

He was just sixteen when Germany invaded Poland. The schools closed, including the Yeshiva he and his two brothers, grandsons of a Hasidic rabbi, attended. Jews were forced into a crowded ghetto. One day soldiers picked up everyone in the street. The imprisoned boy's father asked him to promise to be a good Jew and a good human being.

Forced into hard labor, Simon dug tunnels for a railway near Poznan and then cleared a forest near Andrzejewo. When he returned to the ghetto, his family was gone. He went into hiding, sleeping nights on a grocery table and sneaking over the fence daily to eat with the factory workers. In 1944 the ghetto was emptied. "It was July," Simon recalls. "The sealed train took three days. . . . We stripped off our clothes to cool down. . . . When the doors were finally opened (at Auschwitz), half the people were dead." Months later, as Allied troops advanced, the weak and starving prisoners were forced on a six-week march into Czechoslovakia and Germany. Out of thousands of marchers, only 150 survived to greet American liberators at the Flossenburg concentration camp on April 23, 1945.

Simon, whose family had perished, soon married Mina, a Holocaust survivor, and moved into a confiscated apartment in Regensberg, Germany. They took in Oskar Schindler, his wife, Millie, and his Czech secretary, Marta, and became lasting friends. When Schindler left for Argentina, he offered them passage with Catholic documents, but Simon and Mina resolved to remain Jews.

FRIEDA WEINREICH

Memphis, Tennessee
B.1924, Lodz, Poland
Survivor: Lodz Ghetto; Auschwitz
Concentration Camp; Parschnitz
Slave Labor Camp

"The inmates must have known that she was going to the crematorium. But I just held onto my mother as they dragged me away," says Frieda Weinreich. "I had no idea what was happening, but they knew, and they saved my life. She died in a gas chamber."

Frieda had five brothers and sisters, loving parents, and a home in which she felt safe. Just months after her fifteenth birthday, the security she had known was gone. "The war broke out, and the Germans came to Lodz and began beating people up," she recalls. "Synagogues were burned down; schools for Jewish children were destroyed."

By December 1939, Frieda and her family were in the Lodz ghetto. "Life in the ghetto was cramped," she says. "We had limited food and no coal to heat our home. We were so cold and many people died from starvation." Her father was among them; he died in 1941.

Frieda and others prayed in secret, knowing that their Jewish faith bound them together. They honored the Sabbath in whatever way they could. "We saved potatoes through the year," she recalls, "so that during Passover we could go without bread and still survive."

In 1944, Frieda and her mother were sent to Auschwitz. It was there that fellow prisoners pulled her out of a line headed to the gas chambers. She survived to work as a bricklayer at Parschnitz, a labor camp in Czechoslovakia. Frieda reflects, "I have no idea how I survived long enough to see the Russian soldiers." They arrived on May 9, 1945.

SAM WEINREICH

Memphis, Tennessee
B. 1919, Lodz, Poland
Survivor: Lodz Ghetto; Auschwitz
and Dachau Concentration Camps

"For days I only saw what looked like dead people walking," Sam Weinreich says. "I held tightly to my wooden spoon and bowl. . . . To be caught without it, you could not eat."

At Auschwitz concentration camp, Sam Weinreich labored by day covering corpses with chlorine disinfectant. By night he sang for Nazi doctors for an extra piece of bread. His song—and maybe the bread—kept him alive: "I would sing a particular song that would always make this one Nazi cry."

Sam remembers his home in Poland and his eight brothers and sisters. He remembers the family-run furniture and antique shops. He remembers the piercing shout of a cyclist going door to door warning that the Germans were coming. "I fled to Warsaw to protest the treatment of the Jewish people," he says, "but the city was burning and people were starving. I returned home."

When the Nazis seized his shop, Sam's father lost the ability to support his family. Cold and desperately hungry, they went willingly to what they thought would be a better place: the Lodz ghetto. Sam chopped wood all day for an extra bowl of soup. In 1944, he was deported to Auschwitz. He never saw anyone he knew again.

Later sent to Dachau, Sam managed to escape as he exited the train: "We walked through the forest for weeks. . . . We were hungry. . . . We had just about given up." One morning, as they slept, nearly frozen to death, on a bed of leaves, an American soldier found them. "This American soldier said he would take care of us," he remembers. "I never thought I would live to hear that. Ever."

FRED WESTFIELD

Nashville, Tennessee
B. 1926, Essen, Germany
Refugee

"We were taken to England, and I didn't see my parents for eight long months," recalls Fred Westfield. Even after his parents joined him, Fred says that a sweep of all German-Jewish immigrants in 1940 "sent [his] father to an internment camp. Winston Churchill feared they might be spies."

Fred had boarded a train bound for London in 1939 as part of the *Kindertransport*, a British effort to save Germany's Jewish children from Nazi terror. Thirteen-year-old Fred was placed with a foster family until his parents could safely retrieve him. Weekly letters allowed them to keep in touch.

In 1936, at the first rumblings of civil unrest in Germany, Fred's parents had filed for United States visas. His fifteen-year-old brother had been allowed to emigrate, but Fred, his mother, and his father were trapped by the U.S. quota system, which granted only a certain number of Jewish refugees entry in a given year. The British, however, were accepting Jewish adults who could financially support themselves and would agree not to seek employment. The Westfields were assigned a number and told to wait their turn.

By the time their U.S. visa number came up, Fred's parents were in England, but his father was being detained along with other German nationals. The U.S. visa secured his release, and the family boarded a ship from Liverpool, England, for New York. They were reunited with Fred's brother in Nashville.

144

DEE WOLFE

Erin, Tennessee
B. 1922, Savannah, Tennessee
U.S. Army Witness: Buchenwald
Concentration Camp

Dee Wolfe's military police battalion was ordered to Buchenwald a few days after it was liberated in April 1945. They observed German citizens who were forced to go through the camp. Dee recalls, "It was about two or three miles from the nearby town and the people were made to walk out and observe. Some cried, some didn't have any feelings, anyway they got to see it."

Dee remembers being allowed to walk about freely: "When I went in through the gate I saw on the right a big building . . . with a smokestack that was probably a couple of hundred feet high. . . . When I looked down to my right I saw corpses laying there stacked up like cordwood." He went into the basement, where "I opened the furnace door and found partially burned body parts of people still there." He saw survivors in barracks that looked like chicken houses, "The places where the prisoners were sleeping were about six feet long and fifteen to twenty inches high, just big enough for the prisoners to get in and sleep. There wasn't cover of any kind or anything else and the only thing they had was that little stall, and that's where they stayed and slept."

Dee found it hard to see humans desperate for food and not feed them, "but we'd been given orders not to give them anything so we didn't." Their commanders knew from experience that for dehydrated and starving people, only careful reacclimation to solid food would prevent the intestines from bursting.

HENRY WOLKOFF

Nashville, Tennessee
B. 1914 Lutomiersk, Poland
Survivor: Pabianice and Lodz Ghettos;
Auschwitz, Mauthausen, and Ebensee
Concentration Camps

SALLY ABRAMCZYK WOLKOFF

Nashville, Tennessee
B. 1921 Pabianice, Poland
Survivor: Pabianice and Lodz Ghettos;
Auschwitz, Freiburg, and Mauthausen
Concentration Camps

"She just knows I know and there is comfort in that. We don't have to say anything. We understand the pain. We understand each other," says Henry Wolkoff, who met his wife, Sally, in the Pabianice ghetto.

He continues, "You wanted to talk to other people there. You could learn about what was going on in other places—mostly rumors—and sometimes you made a friend. We would walk together and talk." When the ghetto was closed in 1942 they lost touch. Both were deported to Lodz and then to Auschwitz.

Sally remembers the last time she saw her family together: "It was in line awaiting separation at Auschwitz. Two of my sisters were sent to the airplane factory and my other sister and I were sent for office work." Her father's instructions were, "Whoever survives must return to Poland to find each other."

Henry was sent to the Mauthausen concentration camp and taken by cattle car to Ebensee. Sally survived Freiburg and Mauthausen. She whispers, "It is impossible for me to describe what I saw there at the camps. Death everywhere. Bodies, sickness . . . I just can't explain it." As she confronts the memories, she cries.

At liberation in May 1945, Sally was suffering from starvation and from typhus, a disease caused by lice and crowded, unsanitary living conditions. Henry, too, was sick with typhus. But both made their way back to Poland. When Sally saw Henry again, she says, "I knew he was the man I wanted to marry. I just looked at him and I knew." Henry reaches for her hand. "We don't talk about it. It is very hard for us," he says, bowing his head in memory of family members who did not survive.

INDEX

A

Adler, Herta, xxvi, 2
Akiba, Rabbi, xxx
Aktion, 4
Ambrose, Saint, xx
American-German Distribution
    Committee, 96
Andrzejewo forced labor camp,
    138
Aryan, xxvi–xxvii
Augustine, Saint, xx
Auschwitz-Birkenau concentration
    camp, xix, xxiii, xxxii–xxxiii,
    16, 20, 22, 30, 46, 54, 56, 60, 62,
    64, 66, 70, 86, 90, 96, 116, 122,
    126, 130, 138, 140, 142, 148

B

Bad Orb POW camp, 12
Battle of the Bulge, 12, 42
Belzec death camp, xxiii, 96
Bendzin ghetto, 130
Berga slave labor camp, 12
Bergen-Belsen concentration
    camp, xxiii, 22, 60, 64
Bergen-Belsen displaced persons
    camp, 58, 72
Berger, Ethel, xxxiii, 4
Blank, Mark, 6
Blatteis, Clark, xxvi, 8
Blizyn slave labor camp, 24, 62, 64

blood libel, xx
Borochina, Olga, xxviii, 10
Buchenwald concentration camp,
    xxii, xxxi–xxxii, 48, 74, 80,
    128, 146
Budapest ghetto, 88

C

Carden, Wallace F., 12
Chelmno, xxiii
Chernovtsy ghetto, 68
Chill, Leonard, xxvii, xxix, 14
Chojnacki, Rachel Gliksman,
    xxvi, 16
Chorostkow ghetto, 38
Chrysostom, Saint John, xx
Chust ghetto, 86
Chzanow ghetto, 60
Cohen, Jack, 18
Crusades, xx
Cutler, Frances, xxiii, xxix, 20
Czestochowa ghetto, 58, 74
Czestochowa slave labor camp, 58,
    72, 74

D

Dachau concentration camp, xxii,
    xxix, xxxi, 26, 32, 40, 42, 44,
    46, 52, 62, 66, 82, 100, 124,
    132, 142

death march, 12, 22, 64, 100,
    120, 124, 132, 138
Diament, Henrietta, xxiii, 22
Diamond, Ruth, xxiii, 24
Diez, xxvi, 2
Dorris, Jr., James F., xxxi, 26
Dreyer, Trudy Naumann, 28
Dubois, Sonja, xxiii, xxix, 30

E

Ebensee concentration camp,
    148
Eisenstein, Robert, xxxi, 32
Enlightenment, xix–xxi
Evian converence, xxvi, xxxi
Exelbierd, Joseph, 34
expulsion of Jews, xx

F

Feldafing displaced persons
    camp, 44
Feuerbach, Ludwig, xxi
Fichte, Johann Gottlieb, xx
Final Solution, xxvii, 118
First World War, xxii, 2, 80
Flossenburg concentration camp,
    138
Freiburg concentration camp, 148
Freisig displaced persons camp,
    16

Fribourg, Henry, 36
Fried, Jack, 38
Fürstenfeldbruck airfield, 32

G

Garner, James, xxxi, 40
Geislingen munitions factory, 46
Gentry, Jimmy, 42
German Idealism, xxi
German Workers' Party, xxii
Gestapo, xxvi, 52, 54
Goebbels, Joseph, 50
Gontownik, Zina, xxiii, xxix, 44
Goodfriend, Matilda Steinberg,
    xxii, 46
Göring, Hermann, xxvii, 118
Greece, occupation of, 18
Gregorios of Chalkis, Archbishop,
    18
Gurs concentration camp, 54

H

Halbstadt forced labor camp, 16
Hall, Willie, xxxi, 48
Hamburger, Hanna, 50
Hannsdorf forced labor camp, 56
HASAG munitions factory, 58,
    72, 74
Hegel, G. W. F., xx–xxi
Heidegger, Martin, xxi
Heydrich, Reinhard, xxvii
hidden child, 20, 30, 54, 84, 90,
    94, 122

Hitler, Adolf, xxii–xxiii, xxvi, 40,
    52, 110, 122
Holocaust Remembrance Day,
    xxxiv
Hosnedl, Julian Joseph, 52

I

Israel (name), xxx

J

Jablonica forced labor camp, 38
Jarvis, Fred, xxix, 54

K

Kaiserwald concentration camp,
    44
Kant, Immanuel, xx–xxii
Kapo, 66
Katz, Nina, xxiii, xxvii, xxxii,
    xxxiv, 56
Kelman, Paula, xxix, 58
Kilstein, Ida Frank, 60
Kilstein, Jacob, xxvi, xxxii–xxxiii,
    62
Kimmelman, Mira Ryczke, xxiii,
    xxviii–xxix, 64
Kindertransport, 54, 78, 144
Klagenfurt prison, 52
Klein, William, xxii, 66
Kolbuszowa ghetto, 96
Kovno ghetto, xxix, 84, 100, 132
Kreymerman, Yakov, 68, 136

Kristallnacht, xii, xxvi, 2, 8, 28, 50,
    78, 80

L

Landau, Frida, xxii–xxiii, 70
liberator, xii, xxix, xxxi–xxxiv,
    26, 40, 42, 48, 82, 102, 128,
    148
Limor, Elizabeth, 72
Limor, Menachem, xxii–xxiii,
    74
Lodz ghetto, xxvi–xxvii, 16, 22,
    138, 140, 142, 148
Loeb, Esther, xxxii, xxxvi, 76
Loewenstein, Herman, 78
Lustig, Hedy, 80

M

Majdanek concentration camp,
    xxiii, 22, 24, 64
Mamlin, Robert, xxix, 82
Marks, Nessy, xxix, 84
Marton, Rose, xxiii, 86
Mátészalka ghetto, 46
Mauthausen concentration camp,
    xxii, 88, 130, 148
Messiah, xxix
Messing, George, 88
Messing, Helene, xxiii, 90
Midrash Chinukh, xxix, xxxv
military liaison, 112
Mitelman, Roman, xxxvii, 92
Mogilev-Podolskiy ghetto, 6, 10, 68

Mogilev-Podolskiy concentration camp, 136

Mühldorf underground aircraft factory, 66

Mühldorf-Dachau concentration camp, 44, 66

N

Naft, Lea Slomivic, 120, 126

Narbonne, xx

National Socialist Association of University Lecturers, xxi

National Socialist German Workers' Party (Nazis), xxii

Natzweiler-Struthof concentration camp, xxii, 46

Neusaltz labor camp, 60

Newman, Olivia, 94

Nietzsche, Friedrich, xxi

Nordhausen concentration camp, xxxi, 48, 64, 102

Notowitz, Max, xxiii, xxviii, 96

Nuremberg laws, xxiii, 28, 134

Nuremberg war crimes trial, xii, 112, 118

O

Oberaltstadt slave labor camp, 56

Oks, Reva, 98

P

Pabianice ghetto, 148

Pais, Arthur, xxii, 100

Palestine, 38, 120

Parschnitz slave labor camp, 140

Patton, General George, 82

Pawiak prison, 14

Piotrków ghetto, xxvi, 62

Poznan forced labor camp, 138

Pustkow slave labor camp, 96

R

Radom ghetto, 22

Ravensbrück concentration camp, 52

Ray, Jr., Robert, xxxi, 102

refugee, xxvi, 2, 8, 28, 34, 36, 50,76, 78, 80, 92, 96, 104, 106, 134, 136, 144

Reichstag, xxii

Rivesaltes concentration camp, 54

Romanian Iron Guard, 108, 110, 120

Roosevelt, President Franklin, 106

Rosenberg, Alfred, xxvii

Rosenfeld, Eric, 104

Rosenfeld, Eva, 106

S

SA (Nazi Storm Trooper), 78

Saharovici, Fridericka, 108

Saharovici, Leonid, xxxvi, 110

St. Louis (ship), xxvi, 8

Salzheim displaced persons camp, 16

Sandvig, Raymond, 112

Sarah (name), xxx

Savranskiy, Alexander, 114

Schindler, Oskar, 138

Schlanger, Gertrude, xxiii, 116

Schopenhauer, Arthur, xxi

Schultze, Walter, xxi

Schulz, Ralph, 118

Seidner, Jack, 120

Seidner, Sara Slomovic, 120, 126

Sekernice ghetto, 126

Siberian forced labor camp, 76, 98

Sigel, Erika, xxiii, 122

Silber, Ella, 124

Skarzysko slave labor camp, 72

slaughter of Jews, xx

Snodgrass, Harry, xxii, xxxi–xxxii, 128

Sobibor, xxiii

Society for the Rescue of Jewish Children (OSE), 54

Stanislawow ghetto, 4

Star of David, 10, 84, 122, 124, 126

Stein, Paula, xxii, 130

Stein, Sol, 132

Strupp, Hans, 134

Stutthof concentration camp, xxiii, 44, 100, 124

Stutthof slave labor camp, 126

T

Talmud, xxi, xxix–xxx
Terk, Raisa (Kreymerman), 136
Theresienstadt concentration
    camp, xxii, 70
Thule Society, xxii
Tisha B'Av, xxviii
Tomashpol ghetto, 114
Tomazów-Mazowiecki ghetto,
    64
Torah, xxvii–xxix
Transniester labor camp, 120
Treblinka death camp, xxiii,
    xxvii–xxviii, 74

U

Unsleben, xxvi, 28
Untermenschen, xxi

V

Vatican, xxxi
Voltaire, xx

W

Waksberg, Simon, xxiii, 138
Wannsee conference, xxvii
Warsaw ghetto, xxvi–xxviii, 14,
    22, 64, 66

Weimar Republic, xxii
Weinreich, Frieda, xxiii, xxix,
    140
Weinreich, Sam, xxiii, 142
Westfield, Fred, 144
William of Norwich, xx
Wilno ghetto, xxvii, 14, 44
Windsheim displaced persons
    camp, 34
witness, xxxi, 32, 146
Wolfe, Dee, xxxiii, 146
Wolkoff, Henry, xxii, 148
Wolkoff, Sally Abramczyk, xxii,
    148